Food mania

Bonbonnière

&

Eremitage

Schnackenberg

NIGEL GARWOOD
AND RAINER VOIGT

Food mania

preface by Anton Mosimann

with 482 illustrations

CLARKSON POTTER/PUBLISHERS
New York

Half-title Pudding illustration from *Mrs. Beeton's Book of Household Management*, second and enlarged edition, 1869.

Frontispiece Bonbonnière & Eremildge: poster by Walter Schnackenberg, *c.* 1920. © DACS 2001

This page and *opposite* Illustrations from Jules Gouffé's *Royal Book of Pastry*, 1874.

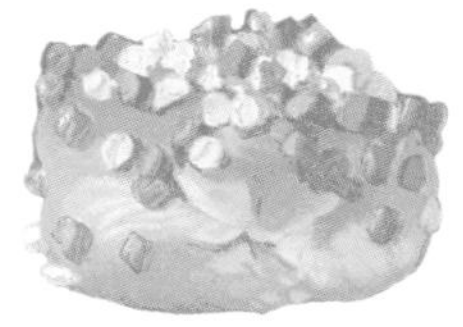

Special photography by Julien Busselle

Published by Clarkson Potter/Publishers
New York, New York
Member of the Crown Publishing Group

Random House, Inc., New York, Toronto, London, Sydney, Auckland

www.randomhouse.com

Clarkson N. Potter is a trademark and Potter and colophon are registered trademarks of Random House, Inc.

Originally published in Great Britain by
Thames & Hudson Ltd., London, in 2001
Printed and bound in China

Library of Congress Cataloging-in-Publication Data
is available upon request from the publisher.

ISBN 0-609-80876-1

10 9 8 7 6 5 4 3 2 1

First American Edition

Contents

Calves Head Jelly
Pancake
Bulls eyes
currant Jelly
Raspberry Jam
Puff-Paste
Ladies fingers
Dough
Puff
Mock Turtle
Lolly-pop
a Trifle
Isinglafs
Duff
wafers
Ladies fingers
White Sugar Bags
Hard Bake
Gilt Gingerbread

Preface

by ANTON MOSIMANN

My philosophies of food and life are the same. They should both be experiences of happiness, serenity and joyful giving. I can still remember the sweet smell of dark, sugared fruit bubbling in the heavy copper preserving pan as my mother made jam. From those early years, when my parents ran a farm and a restaurant, whilst I sat doing my homework in the restaurant kitchen, I would watch them chopping vegetables, cooking braised beef, rabbit or veal, and preparing sauces with such enthusiasm and passion. I knew then I would be a chef.

Today the subject of food is constantly on people's lips. There are hours of television programmes dedicated to food. Every newspaper and magazine features a food column and has its own restaurant critic, who tells its readers what is good, bad or just plain indifferent. Cookery books abound on the shelves of bookshops.

This delightful book, with its montage of paintings, photographs and illustrations, traces its way through the history of food. It is a truly eclectic collection, capturing with charm some unusual aspects of food from the gathering, preparation and dressing of it. *Food Mania* will be an inspiration to anyone, both professional cooks and enthusiastic amateurs.

Opposite Sugar and spice: broadsheet by George Cruikshank, 1818.

Introduction: Food Mania

Maintaining the food supply is one of the paramount human concerns: food is life and we have to ensure that we have constant supplies of it. We have to locate it, prepare it, serve it and eat it. Each one of these stages is reflected in the images from several centuries and countries which make up the major part of this book. In assembling this collection of illustrations, we found the diversity of subject-matter quite astonishing: from representations of harvests, the plenty of the market, the still-life quality of food in the larder, the frenzy of the kitchen, to the elaborate rituals, equipment and settings which attend the actual consumption of food – perhaps the easiest part of the whole chain to illustrate, but certainly the one most susceptible to manic behaviour. It is, indeed, the arts of the table – or other eating surface – which inspire the most elaborate declared and undeclared ritual complexity in our relationship with comestibles.

Opposite and *this page* front of menu card and details: design by Jacques Touchet for the Compagnons de la Belle Table, 1948.

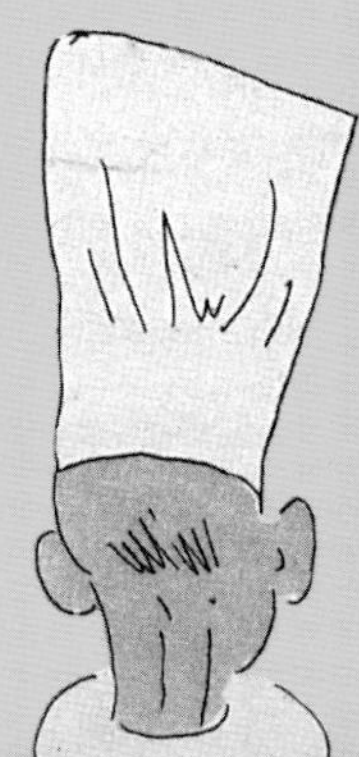

Above 'Two monks at supper': anonymous late nineteenth-century painting.

Opposite Illustrations from Jules Gouffé's *Le Livre de cuisine*, Paris, 1867.

One image wonderfully illustrative of food mania, the contrast between obesity and thinness (page 374), by the nineteenth-century French illustrator Bertall, is drawn from a particularly splendid edition of the greatest work on food mania of modern times, *La Philosophie du goût* by Jean-Anthelme Brillat-Savarin, originally published in 1825. This engaging collection of musings, meditations and maxims on gastronomy identifies the sense of taste as being central to the human experience, inspiring us to ever greater ingenuity in the production, selection and preparation of everything which can be safely consumed via the mouth. His differentiation of gourmandism, the civilized preparation and consumption of food and drink, from sheer gluttony, indiscriminate eating and imbibing, is masterly. His descriptions of excess are a marvellous evocation of a time when massive appetites were considered a sign

of health and well-being rather than a manic obsession with filling one's belly.

The author's visit to a village *curé*, a man renowned for the magnitude of his appetite, is described with admiration. By midday, this good man of the cloth would have already put away the soup and boiled beef courses, followed by a leg of mutton and a capon, both eaten down to the bone, and a 'copious' salad, consumed to the bottom of the serving plate. This was followed by a large white cheese, from which our glutton cut a ninety-degree wedge. The whole was washed down with a bottle of wine and a jug of water. Mania, indeed!

In contrast to such self-indulgence, the author regards true *gourmandise* as one of the great activating forces of the universe: it is *gourmandise* which drives the transport of drinks and foodstuffs of all kinds 'from one pole to the other', it sustains the hopes of fishermen, huntsmen and farmers (to which the images in this book are ample testimony); and it is *gourmandise* which gives employment to the 'industrious multitude' of cooks, confectioners, bakers and all concerned with the preparation of foodstuffs. In other words, *gourmandise* is a justifiable mania, so much so that it is even becoming in women. There is no prettier sight, according to Jean-Anthelme, than a good-looking woman displaying a neatly folded napkin, resting one hand on the table while the other lifts dainty morsels, perhaps the wing of a partridge, to her mouth.

As we assembled our collection of gastronomic imagery, of which the selection in this book is but a fraction, it was often said to us that we would find little significant illustration of the cultivation, preparation and consumption of food before the twentieth century. In fact, we found a wealth of material from the eighteenth and nineteenth centuries, much of it incorporating human interest, with distinct differences in its gender associations. Men are generally connected with meat, while women are associated with fruit and vegetables, the preparation of dairy products, and the rearing of poultry. A meat extract factory was clearly man's work in the nineteenth century, but more modern table manners demand a gentler, more 'feminine' approach from the male contingent at a dinner party, a far cry from the rumbustious behaviour of the eighteenth century or the stern paterfamilias of the Victorian era, amply illustrated in our final chapter on the formal meal.

Fashion, national and racial differences and practices, of course, have always dictated what and how we eat once we have advanced beyond the basic level of merely feeding ourselves. Much of the imagery in this book is drawn from a time when excess was considered the norm and *grande cuisine* its highest expression, when Carême prepared his splendid banquets for Talleyrand or, later, when Escoffier ruled over the Paris Ritz or the London Carlton. But change has always been an aspect of our intimate, manic relationship with food, to the point that neophilia is now a way of gastronomic life, from *nouvelle cuisine* to the introduction of various cuisines formerly eschewed as 'ethnic'. Although not illustrated here, such obsession with the new and the fashionable is yet another manifestation of the manic in our relationship with food – the new age of the 'foodie'.

The concluding section of our survey is made up mainly of the imagery of the table, the ultimate expression of our pursuits of happiness (and survival) through food. By 'table' we may understand everything from the final version of the food to be eaten to the actual setting – the table itself, the room in which it stands, the tableware which adorns it, and the people who are gathered around it. In middle-class households the table itself and its accompanying crockery and silverware are often among a family's most prized possessions; Japanese families hold their crockery in especial esteem.

Our old favourite Brillat-Savarin saw gastronomy as the force which makes things tick (‘*qui inspecte les hommes et les choses*’) and as its most sublime expression the well-ordered banquet, the microcosm of the world in which every element is represented. The formal meal at table is the apotheosis of the whole process of the cultivation and rearing, the distribution, and the preparation of food. The table is a special place in the way that the enclosed formal garden is special: it is the encapsulation of the good life, a symbol of the cosmos and of paradise. A full meal is like life itself, beginning with the ‘starter’ (childhood), passing to the main courses (growth and middle age) and ending with pudding and coffee, that final indication that the feast has come to an end. Indeed, like the meal the whole food chain is a process of birth, nurturing and education, full-flowering, with the final dénouement when the last items are removed from the eating place.

Designs for tableware: catalogue by Powell, Bishop and Stonier, London, 1891.

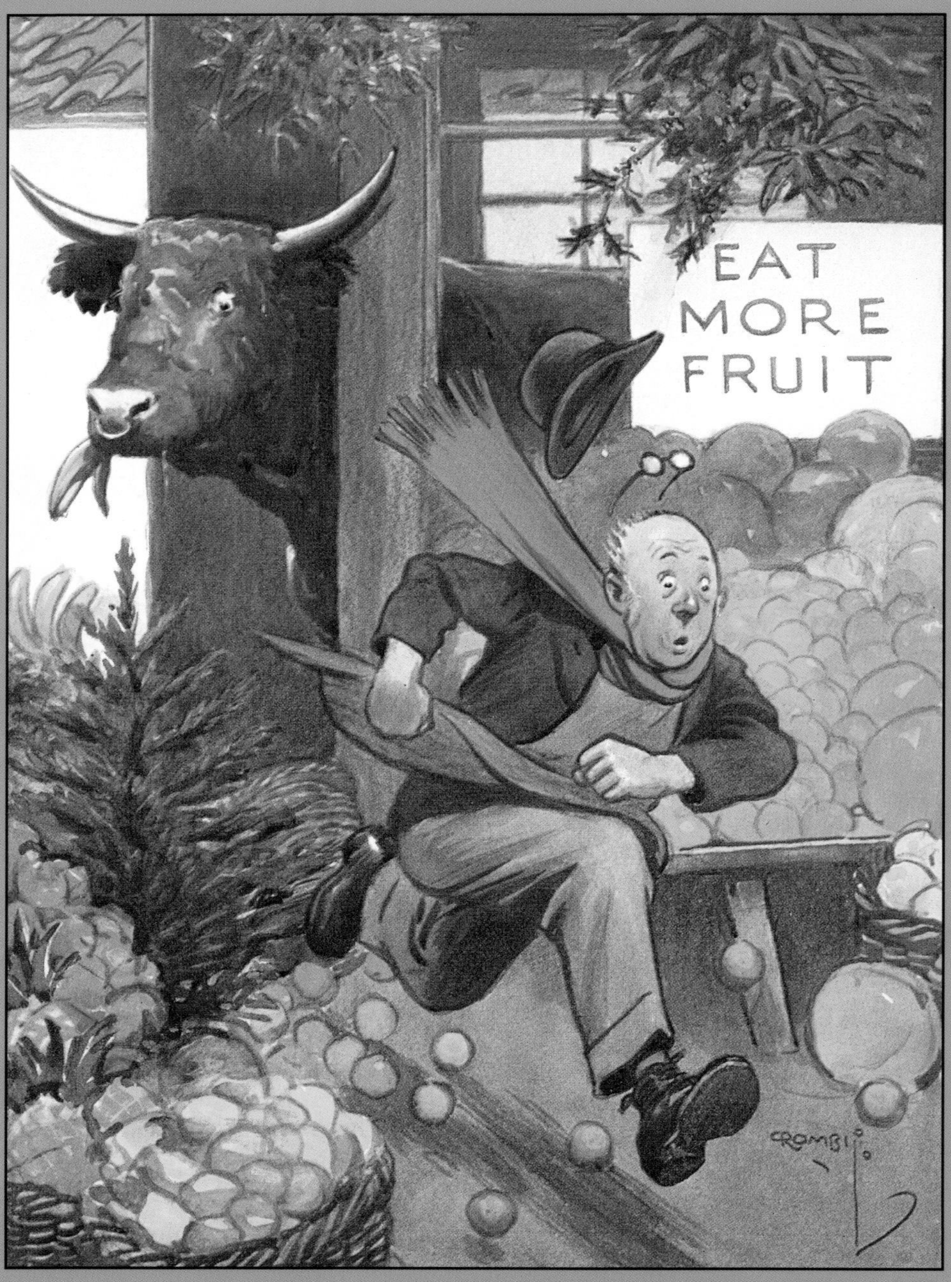
EAT
MORE
FRUIT
CROMBIE

—1—

To Market, To Market

Produce from Farm and Fishing Ground

The growing, rearing and processing of foodstuffs seems to have held a peculiar fascination for the illustrators of the nineteenth century. Popular publications in the major Western capitals frequently published special plates showing the growing, harvesting and refining of 'exotic' crops in distant places. The Caribbean region, especially, provided much newsworthy subject-matter, mainly because the so-called civilized world was dependent on production there of many of its principal luxuries: coffee, cocoa, indigo, tobacco and sugar. The latter, particularly, makes repeated appearances in the pages of the Victorian reviews – plantations, harvesting and refining all minutely illustrated, presumably because the pursuit of 'sweetness' is one of the dominant food manias. Indeed, the production of sugar over the centuries shows the steepest upward curve of any of the major foodstuffs on the world market.

Opposite 'Eat More Fruit': colour print by William Crombie, 1927.

This page Details from a c. 1880 chromolithograph (see pp. 84-85).

The imagery of this chapter, then, is concerned with the growing, rearing and eventual distribution of foodstuffs: the kitchen garden, the farm and plantations, the fruits of field and orchard, the fruits of the sea, and then the market and shop.

Whether one of the great city markets, like Covent Garden, Les Halles, or the splendid one near the Rialto in Venice, or a village or country-town market in, say, Tuscany or Provence, a market impresses by the richness of its display. The elements of this may vary from place to place, from region to region, but 'plenty' is the defining characteristic of what we recognize as the authentic market. We eagerly expect a cornucopia of fruit, vegetables, meat and fish, and all other desirable foodstuffs, promising future delights in larder and kitchen, and at table.

In France, Elizabeth David – surely the greatest English writer on food matters – found everything she considered a market should be. That of Cavaillon in Provence, for instance, excited her powers of culinary observation by its plethora of

Opposite and *this page* A late nineteenth-century market scene; and *(above)* the return home from market, *c.* 1800.

local melons and asparagus, strawberries, redcurrants, cherries, apricots, peaches, pears and plums. Specialist markets, too, figure extensively in these pages – prize-winners at Smithfield in London and quay-side fish markets in the Netherlands.

In spite of the concentration of food distribution and retailing in fewer and fewer hands, mainly the major supermarkets, the image of the market, preferably with an overwhelming display of fresh and colourful produce, retains a powerful hold on the gastronomic imagination. Part of this continuing appeal of a very traditional institution is the very contemporary concern with freshness and variety. Even the fruit and vegetable display-counters of large supermarkets now attempt to ape the atmosphere of country-town markets. But let us hope that the original model never disappears.

Overleaf Fruit picking: copper engraving from Florinus' *Œconomus Prudens*, Nuremberg, 1702.

Above and *below* Details from *The Herefordshire Pomona*, Hereford and London, 1876–85.

Left Fruit picking: chromolithograph, Germany, *c.* 1880.

"LEMON PIPPINS"
"HANWELL SOURING"
"IRISH GIANT"
"POMEROY"
"ASHMEAD'S DESERTS"
"DUCKSBILL"
"LONDON PIPPIN" (?)
HARRISON'S "ANNIE ELIZABETH"
93
VISITORS ARE REQUESTED NOT TO TOUCH THE FRUIT *
GOLDEN SPIRE
CATSHEAD
* ONE REASON
* ANOTHER
"LORD DERBY" – "SIBERIAN" & "AMERICAN CRABS"
"BLACK JACK"
"LADY'S FINGER"
"EH THAT'S LORD DERBY – 'XACTLY"
"WILL THE COMMITTEE NAME THIS SPECIMEN?"
"THE APPLE OF HIS EYE"
POINTERS AT THE APPLE SHOW
A C CORBOULD

Opposite Sketches at the Chiswick Apple Congress: wood engraving from *The Illustrated London News*, 1883.

Right Picking apples: etching by Thomas Riley, 1882.

Autumn treasures: engraving by Claude-Joseph Pomel after Hubert de Genève, Paris, *c.* 1820.

White grapes: plate from Pierre-Joseph Redouté's *Choix des plus belles fleurs...des plus beaux fruits*, Paris, 1827–33.

F.P.sc

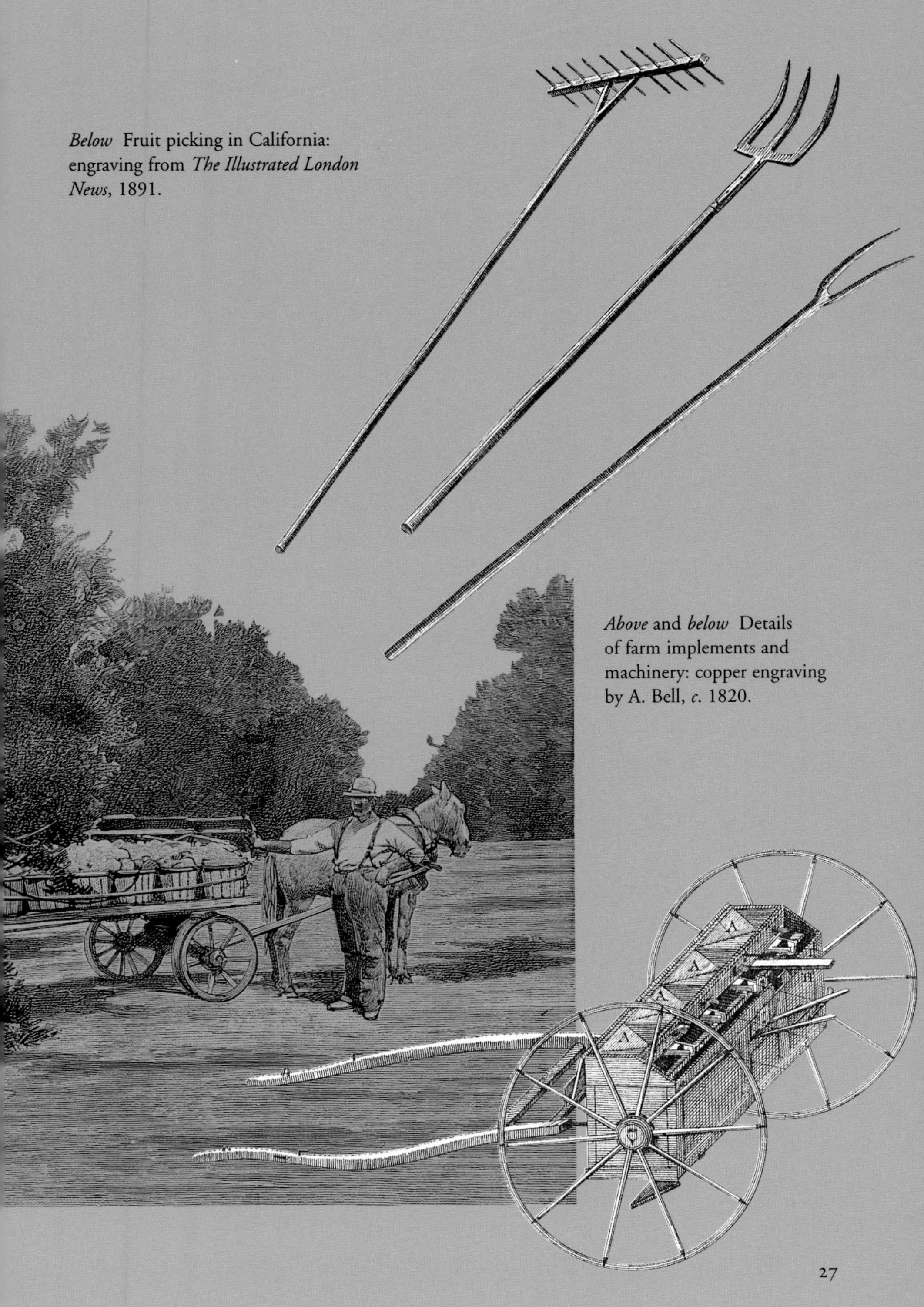

Below Fruit picking in California: engraving from *The Illustrated London News*, 1891.

Above and *below* Details of farm implements and machinery: copper engraving by A. Bell, *c.* 1820.

Produce for the market: chromolithograph, *c.* 1880.

b
d
a
c
u
y
w
t
q
r
t
s

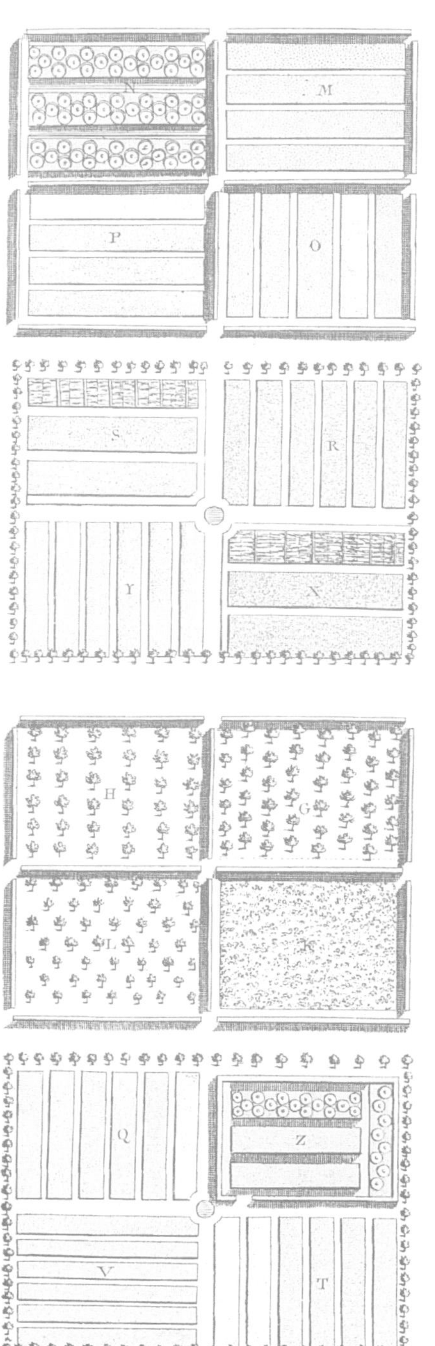

Left Plans for forcing beds in a French *potager*: copper engraving, *c.* 1760.

Above A Greek monastery vegetable garden; copper engraving by A. Walker, *c.* 1762.

Above The corn harvest: chromolithograph, Germany, *c.* 1880.

Right Details of corn types: wood engraving from *The Illustrated London News*, 1860.

Below and *overleaf* Harvest scenes: engravings from Florinus' *Œconomus Prudens*, Nuremberg, 1702.

These pages German illustrations of milling and workers in the field, *c.* 1850; details of farm implements from a French engraving, late eighteenth century.

Above and *below* The traditional harvest of Kent: the interior of an oast-house and a scene from the hop field: wood engraving from *The Illustrated Times*, 1851.

Above The life and times of hop pickers – sketches of life during the hop harvest in Kent: wood engraving from *The Illustrated London News*, 1885.

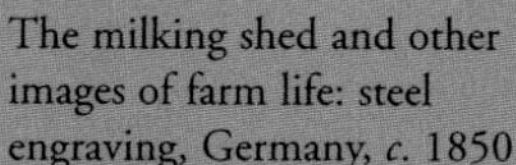

The milking shed and other images of farm life: steel engraving, Germany, *c.* 1850.

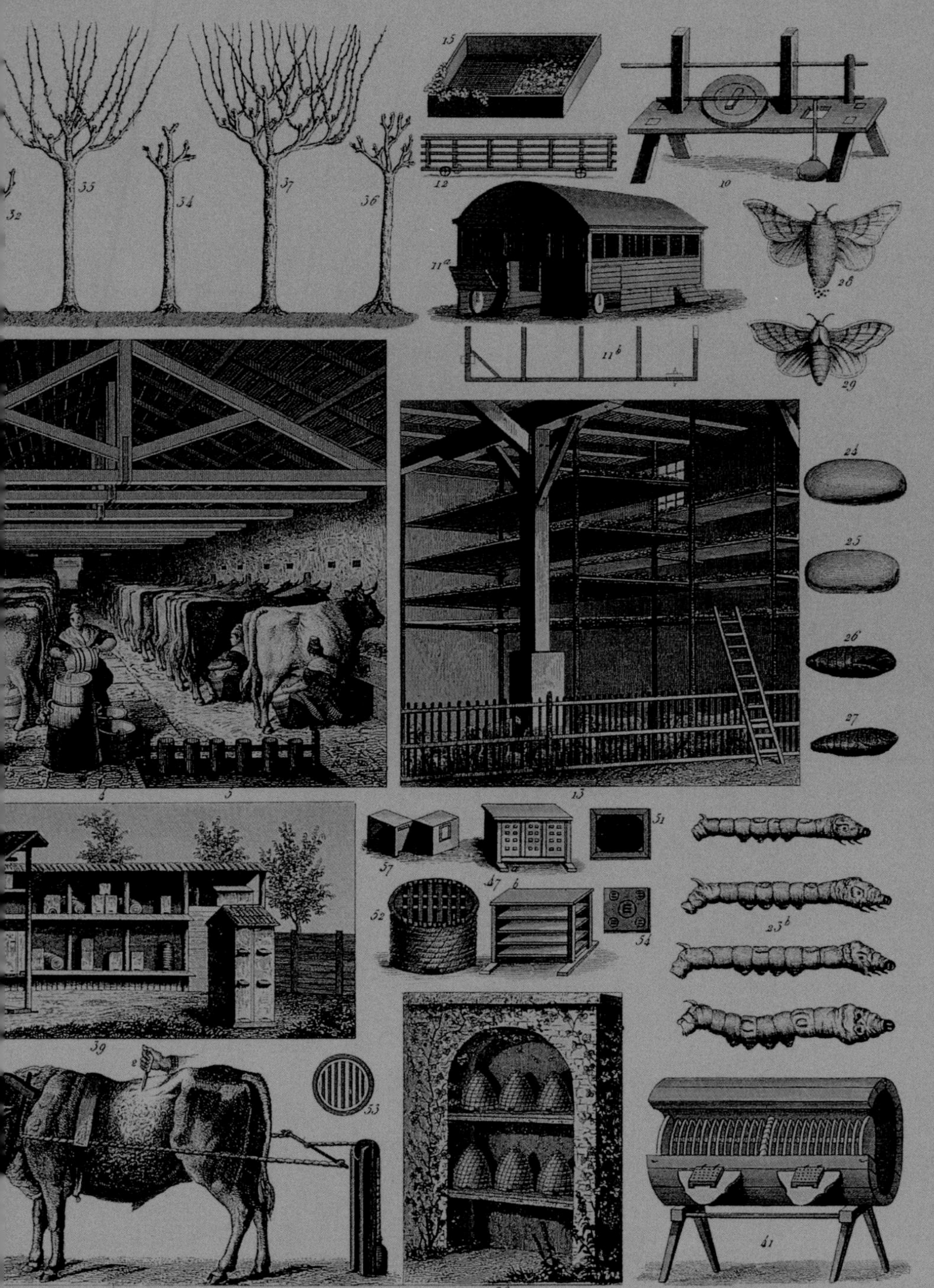

32
35
34
37
36
15
12
10
28
29
24
25
26
27
13
51
57
47
52
54
53
39
1
38
41

Above The olive harvest in Italy: anonymous engraving from *The Illustrated Times*, 1862.

Opposite The olive harvest and oil press on the Riviera: wood engraving by C. I. Durham from *The Illustrated London News*, 1874.

Olive Harvest on the Riviera
Coast between Villa-Franca and Bordechera
E.S.A.
Tête du Chien, Monaco
Interior of Oil Mill
Oil Mill
Gathering Olives
C. I. Durham

A LA MODE BEEF
Envy not unmixed with admiration.
The right sort Marm.
Expectancy

This page Scenes around the market: zinc engraving of drawings by A. L. Molinari, c. 1840; a drayman and horses *(top right)*: original etching by G. W. Rhead, 1887, after a painting by G. F. Watts, R. A.

A Parisian lemonade-seller: wood engraving from *The Illustrated Times*, 1865, after a drawing by Gavarni.

HEARSONS PATENT
HEARSONS PATENT
INCUBATOR
HEARSONS FOSTER MOTHER

Opposite At a poultry farm: wood engraving from *The Illustrated London News*, 1887.

Above From poultry farm to market: wood engraving from *The Illustrated Times*, 1859.

Below Mealtime: etching by R. W. Macbeth, A.R.A., 1882.

Opposite 'October': plate from a nineteenth-century calendar in the style of an illuminated manuscript.

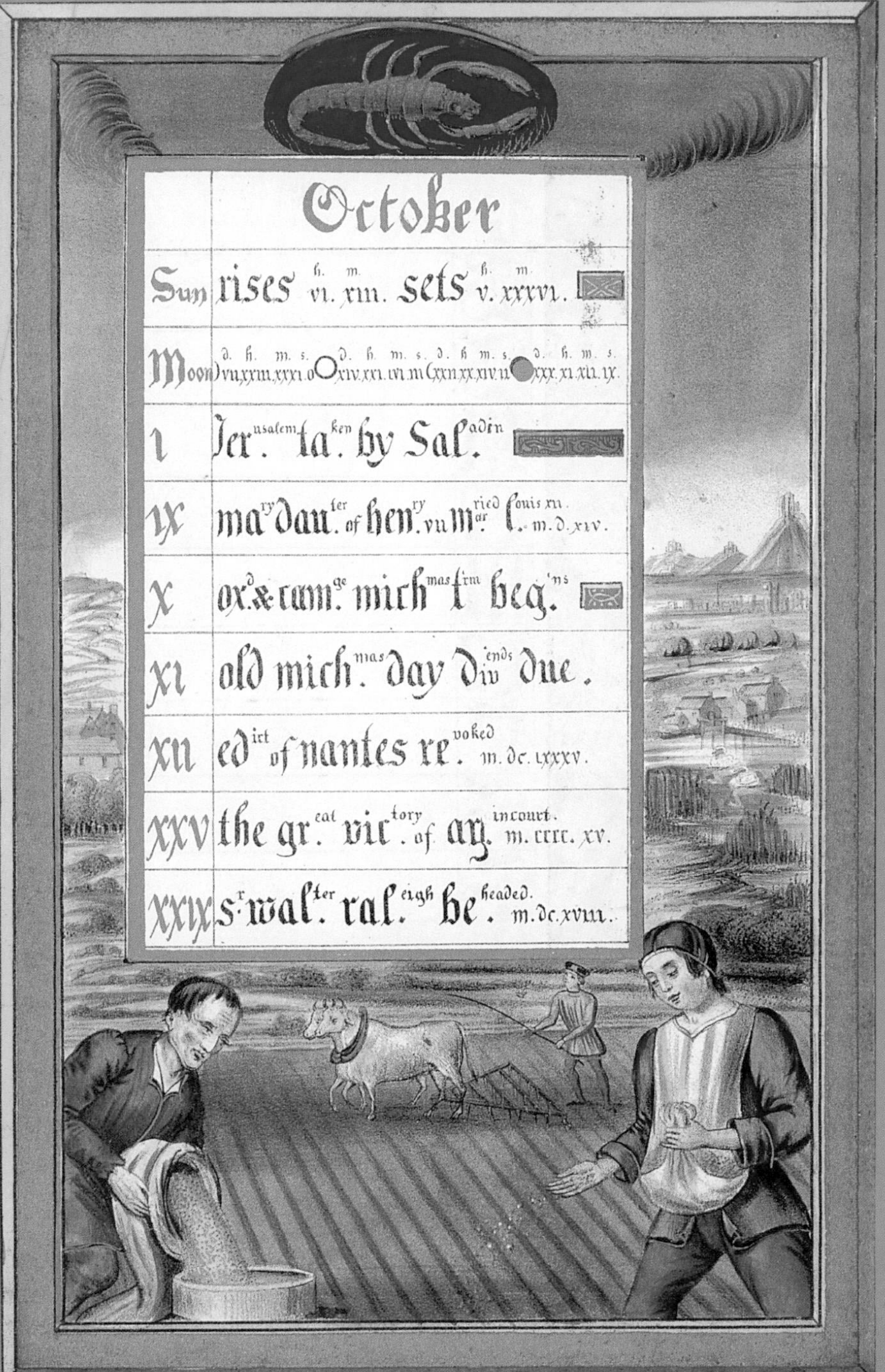

October
Sun rises h. m. vi. xiii. sets h. m. v. xxxvi.
Moon d. h. m. s. vii. xxiii. xxxi. o d. h. m. s. xiv. xxi. lvi. iii d. h. m. s. xxii. xx. xiv. ii d. h. m. s. xxx. xi. xii. ix.
i Jer.usalem ta.ken by Sal.adin
ix ma.ry dau.ter of hen.ry vii mar.ried louis xii. m. d. xiv.
x ox.d & camb.ge mich.mas t.rm beg.ins
xi old mich.mas day div.ends due.
xii ed.ict of nantes re.voked m. dc. lxxxv.
xxv the gr.eat vic.tory of ag.incourt. m. cccc. xv.
xxix sr wal.ter ral.eigh be.headed. m. dc. xviii.

Opposite 'The milk girl': illustrations from a German children's magazine, 1832.

Above Prize exhibits at the Smithfield Club Cattle Show: wood engraving from *The Illustrated London News*, 1867.

Two Types
Country Cousins
From the Highlands
Cecil Aldin
93

Opposite The champion and his admirers at the Smithfield Club Cattle Show: wood engraving by Cecil Aldin, from *The Illustrated London News*, 1893.

Above The village shop – a little bit of everything: chromolithograph from *A Children's Book of Shops*, *c.* 1900.

These pages The farmyard: copper engraving from Florinus' *Œconomus Prudens*, Nuremberg, 1702.

Below 'Can we afford it?' – a goose for Christmas: wood engraving by G. King from *The Illustrated London News*, 1883.

The farmyard's extended family: chromolithograph, Germany, *c.* 1880.

Below 'Spoilt for choice' – Leadenhall Market at Christmas: wood engraving by Harral from *The Graphic*, 1884.

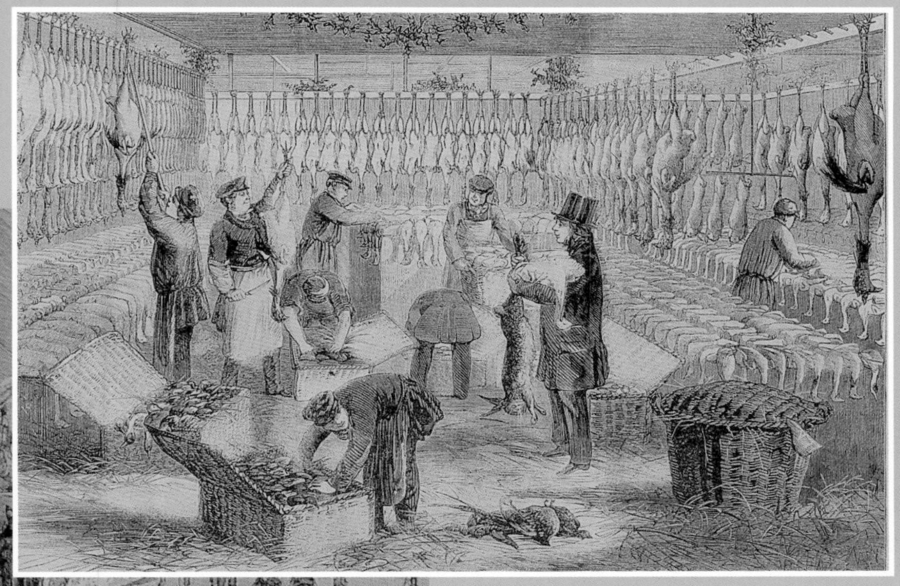

Above Unpacking game and poultry: wood engraving from *The Illustrated Times*, 1859.

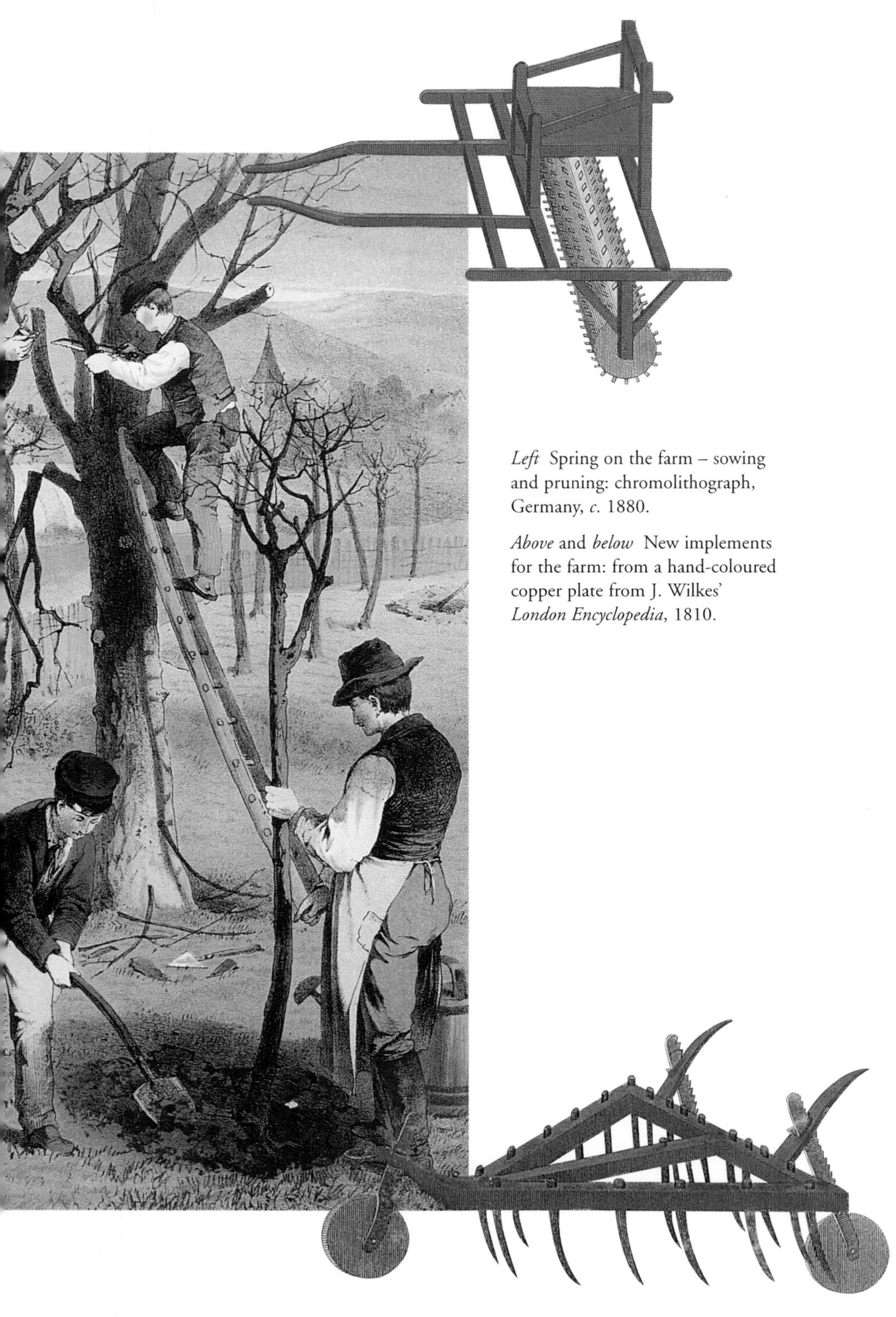

Left Spring on the farm – sowing and pruning: chromolithograph, Germany, *c.* 1880.

Above and *below* New implements for the farm: from a hand-coloured copper plate from J. Wilkes' *London Encyclopedia*, 1810.

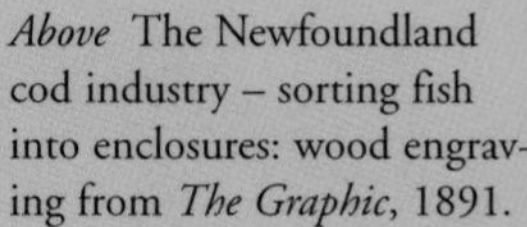

Above The Newfoundland cod industry – sorting fish into enclosures: wood engraving from *The Graphic*, 1891.

Left Billingsgate Fish Market, London: wood engraving by G. Renniand, from *The Illustrated London News*, 1886.

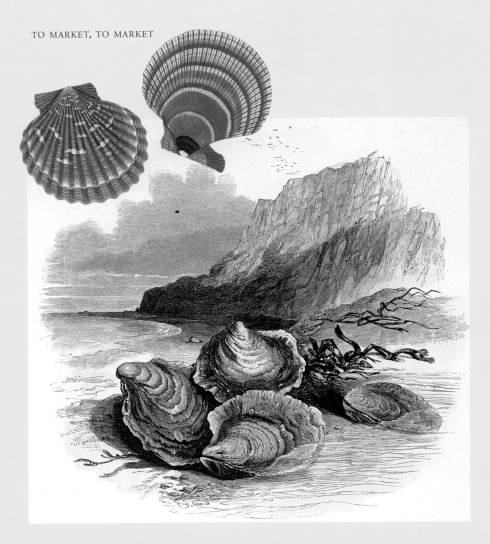

Above The oyster: wood engraving, published by the Committee of General Literature and Education, appointed by the Society for the Promotion of Christian Knowledge, *c.* 1850.

Top and *below* A selection of scallops: copper engraving from J. Wilkes' *London Encyclopedia*, 1810.

Opposite 'Beauties of the Deep': colour illustration by Arthur Hopkins, from *The Graphic*, Summer Number, 1882.

Above Hunting, shooting and fishing: illustration by Bertall from an edition (1848) of Jean-Anthelme Brillat-Savarin's *La Physiologie du goût*, originally published in 1825.

A Surrey trout farm: wood engraving from *The Illustrated London News*, 1890.

Freshly caught salmon and trout: hand-coloured steel engraving by John Miller after J. Stewart, *c.* 1840.

Overleaf The nets: copper engraving from Florinus' *Œconomus Prudens*, Nuremberg, 1702.

Mr. Shrimpton, the fishmonger: chromolithograph by F. D. Bedford from *The Children's Book of Shops*, *c.* 1900.

Overleaf Sorting the catch of the day: steel engraving by J. Kovatisch, *c.* 1840, after a painting by Jacob Jordaens; a Dutch fishwife sells the catch on the quayside *(inset)*: steel engraving, *c.* 1850.

SHRIMPTON · FISHMONGER ·

James Street
Commit no Nuisance

Market traders have fun in Covent Garden Market, London: aquatint by George Cruikshank, *c.* 1840.

Opposite The cheese market at Edam in The Netherlands: engraving by J. Finnemore from *The Sphere*, 1901.

Above The Dutch chestnut-seller: engraving by Caspar Luyken, early eighteenth century.

Victor Gilbert

Opposite *'Convoitise'*, the objects of his desire: colour print from *Le Figaro illustré*, 1900.

Above A London market on Christmas Eve: chromolithograph by J. C. Dollman from *Pears' Christmas Annual*, 1896.

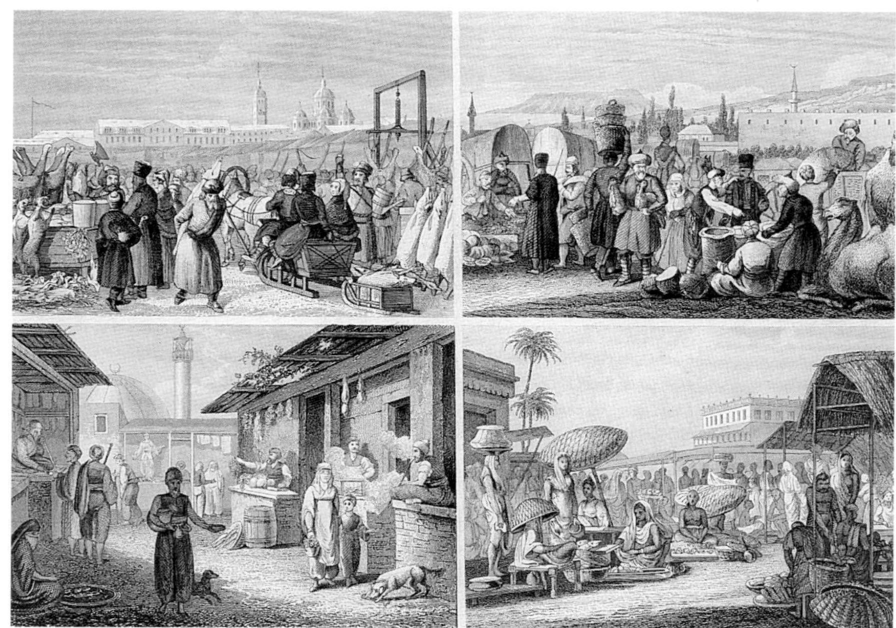

Above Market scenes from Russia, Tartary, Turkey and the East Indies: steel engraving, Germany, *c.* 1850.

Opposite The fig industry in Smyrna, showing sorting weighing, packing and boxing for export: engraving from *The Graphic*, 1886.

1
2
3
4
5

Opposite The fruits of the earth: chromolithograph, *c.* 1880.

Right The cherry-seller in the traditional costume of Hamburg: engraving, *c.* 1790.

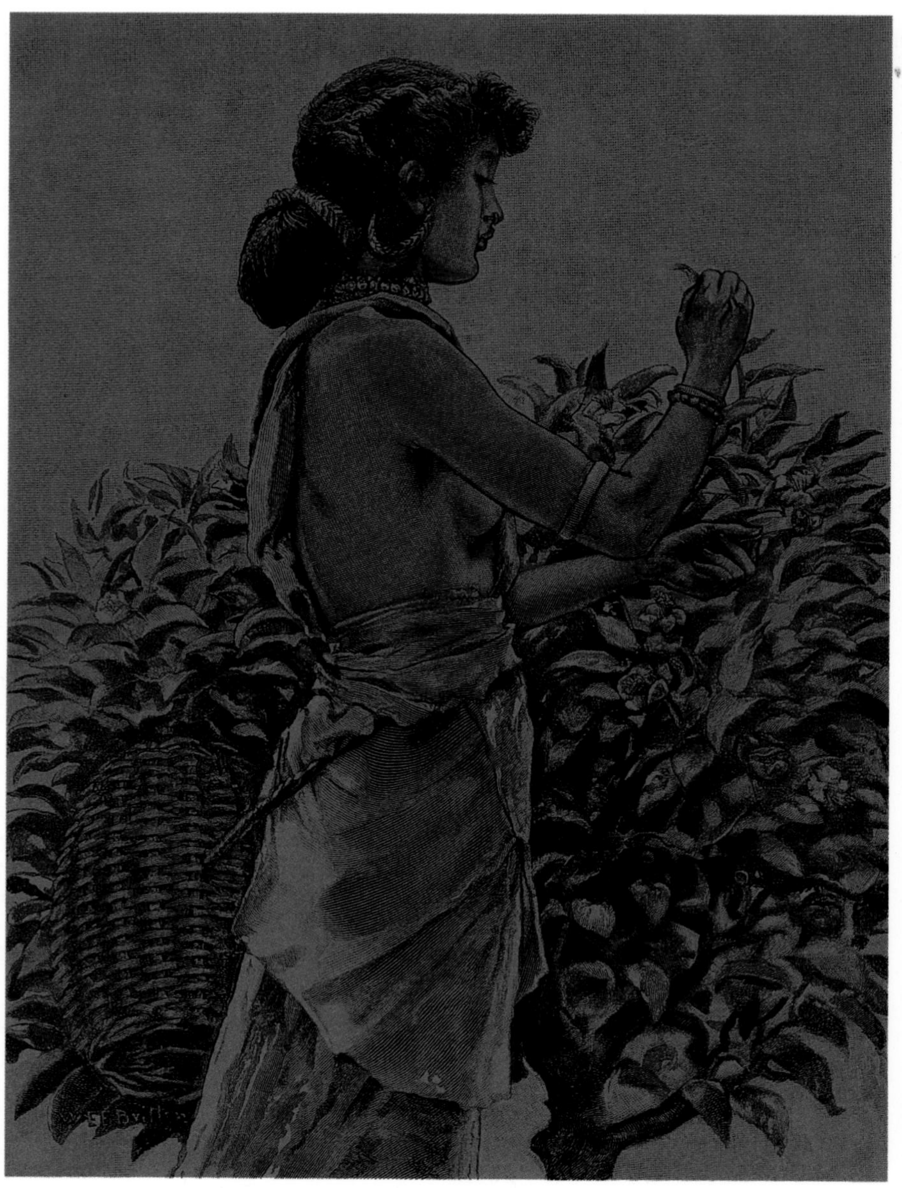

Above The Ceylon tea industry – a Tamil girl plucking a tea bush: wood engraving from *The Graphic*, 1886.

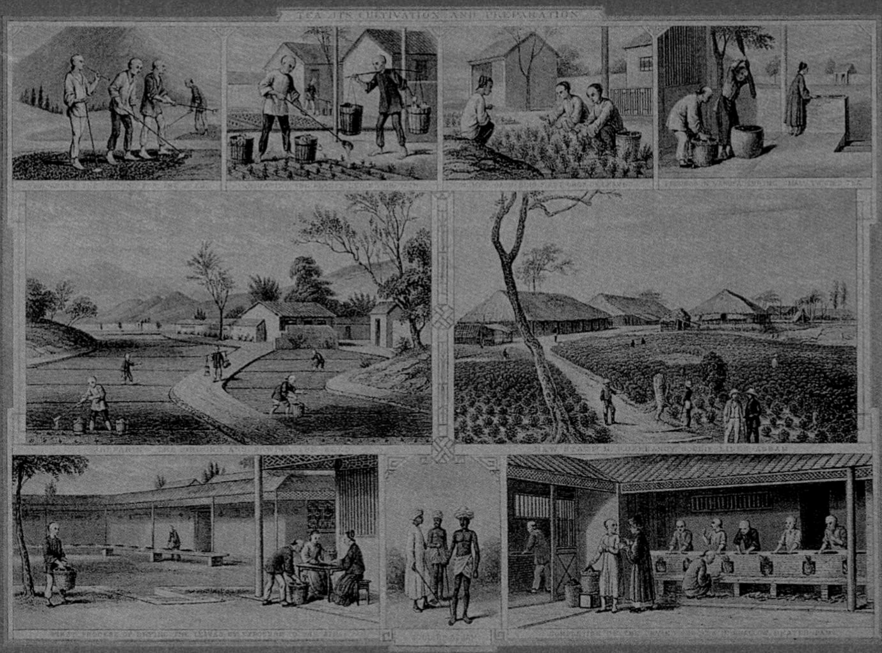

Above Tea cultivation and preparation: tinted engraving by Thomas Brown after J. L. William, *c.* 1860.

Below Coffee, chocolate and tea plants: wood engravings, *c.* 1880.

Opposite above Chinese workers picking, sorting and packing tea: chromolithograph, Germany, *c.* 1880.

Opposite below The coffee plant: from a chromolithograph, *c.* 1860.

Below Harvesting sugar cane in the West Indies: chromolithograph, Germany, *c.* 1880.

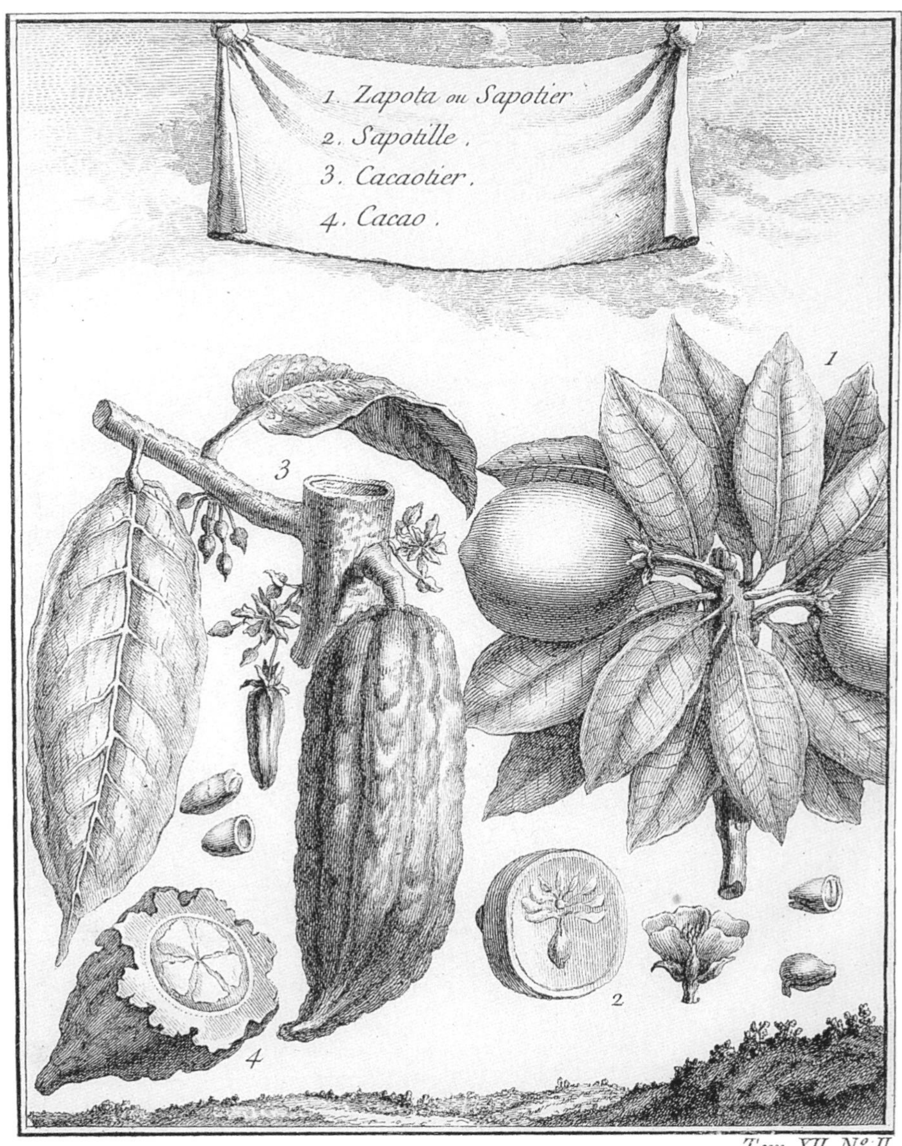

Above Cocoa pods, flowers and seeds: copper engraving from *L'Histoire générale des voyages*, Paris, 1756–61.

Above Cocoa plantation and mill on Grenada, West Indies: wood engraving from *The Illustrated London News*, 1855.

Below Gathering sugar cane and sugar-making: copper engraving from *The Universal Magazine*, *c.* 1750.

Opposite 'In the fruit market of Rio': wood engraving by George Leighton from *The Illustrated London News*, 1856.

Right The apricot: a plate from Redouté's *Choix des plus belles fleurs...des plus beaux fruits*, Paris, 1827–33.

Below The coffee plantation: chromolithograph, Germany, *c.* 1880.

Below Carrying produce, notably bananas, to the market in Kingston, Jamaica: wood engraving from *The Illustrated London News*, 1885.

Above and *below* Counting and collecting bananas in Jamaica for eventual transport to the Kingston market: wood engravings from *The Illustrated London News*, 1885.

—2—

The Butcher, The Baker, The Brewer

Retailing and Refreshment

Appearing here and there among the pages of this book are images of harvesting and food preparation drawn from a series of cards issued by the Liebig Meat Extract Company. Their gastronomic subject-matter ranges from the gathering of exotic crops in far-distant locations to the illustration of kitchens and food preparation. The story behind the cards is one of the most remarkable in the history of deliberate human intervention in the food chain, to which the main body of illustration in this chapter is devoted.

Baron Justus von Liebig, a German professor of chemistry, launched his beef extract – *Extractum Carnis*, as he called it – on the European market in 1865, claiming that one pound of extract had the nutritional equivalent of 40 pounds of meat. In spite of strong evidence that beverages made from the extract amounted to little more than a warm, comforting beef tea, with very little dietary importance, the idea of beef extract as an independent source of

Opposite A German cellarman checks his beer: hand-coloured lithograph showing the character of 'Fritz' in the musical drama *Hermann und Dorothea*, Berlin, *c.* 1860.

Above One of a series of colour cards promoting the products of the Liebig Meat Extract Company, *c.* 1912.

nourishment and as an additive to household cuisine took hold, aided by vigorous advertising and ancillary promotion, like the cards. Even Stanley, setting out to search for Livingstone in the heart of Africa, is reported to have taken some jars of Liebig with him. Soon, there were imitators, especially in the United Kingdom, where the long-enduring Bovril brand had been launched by the late nineteenth century. In Chicago, the Humour Company produced Vigoral, claiming superior 'real meat' content to that in the Liebig product.

Other images in the book, usually featuring healthy-looking livestock or suggesting vigorous growth in humans, testify to the prolonged assault by the extract manufacturing companies and their advertising agencies on the food-buying public.

The pages which follow, then, are essentially about transformation, about changing the results of cultivation and husbandry into products which may very well find themselves lodged, for a time at least, in larder or storeroom. In the bakery or the brewery we find ourselves somewhere between cultivation, the immediacy of market and shop display and the eventual transfer to the domestic or institutional interior.

Above A butcher's window display: chromolithograph from a German manual of shop presentation, *c.* 1912.

The butcher prepares his cuts of meat, the baker transforms his flour into loaves and the brewer provides the wherewithal to wash down the resulting comestibles.

In preparing this section we noticed that the trade of confectioner seems to have been held in peculiar esteem by authors of the early nineteenth century. One writer on cookery and the 'fashionable life', Frederic Nutt, published *The Complete Confectioner* in 1809, including ten engraved plates, 'on the whole art of Confectionery, made easy; with Receipts for Liqueurs, home-made Wines etc...' A more splendid publication appeared in its third edition in Paris in the same year: Madame Utrecht-Friedel's *Le Confiseur Impérial*, with a magnificent engraved frontispiece of the interior of the confectioner's workroom and further plates of confectioners' utensils. The contents are mouth-watering simply by name: 'Les Confitures, Conserves, Gelées, Marmelades .... Biscuits, Fruits à l'eau de vie...Glaces, la Limonade, le Thé, le Chocolate et le Café.' Equally enticing images follow.

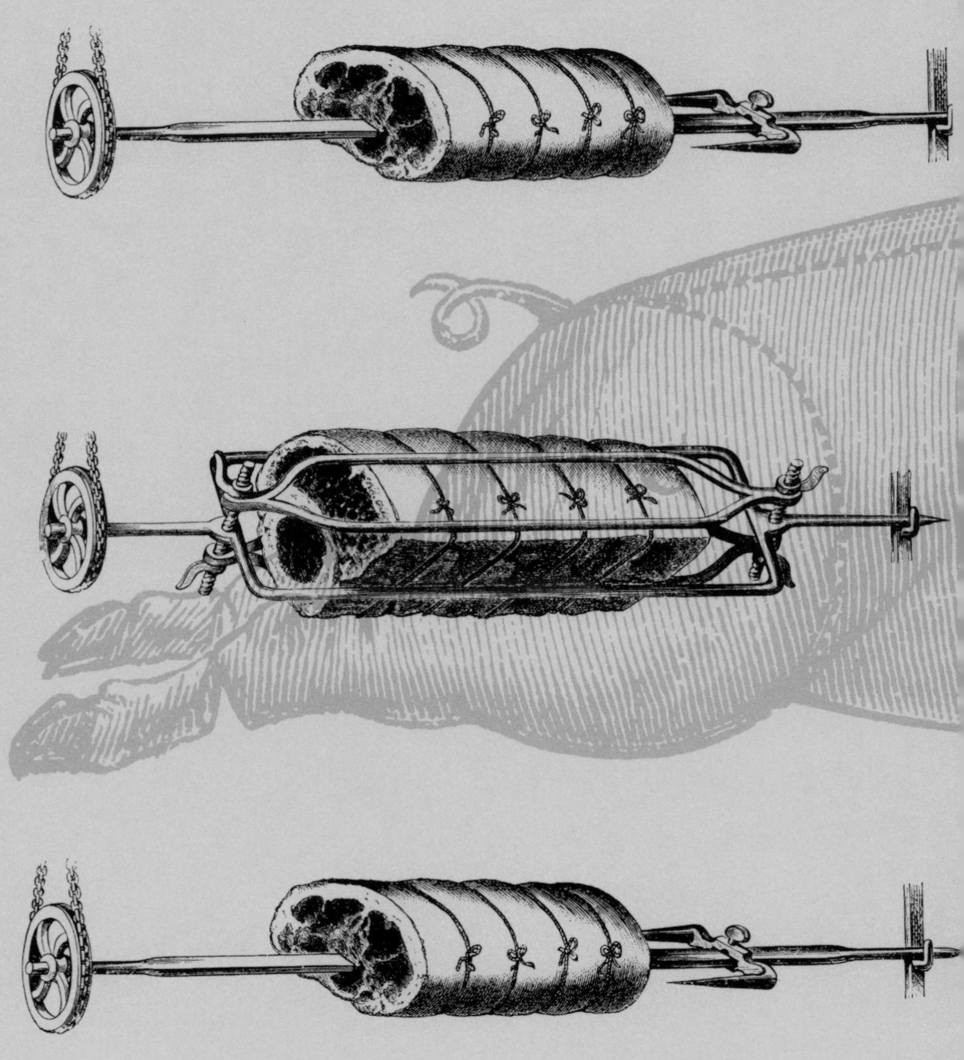

These pages The pork butcher's art: images from nineteenth-century manuals on cutting and roasting pork.

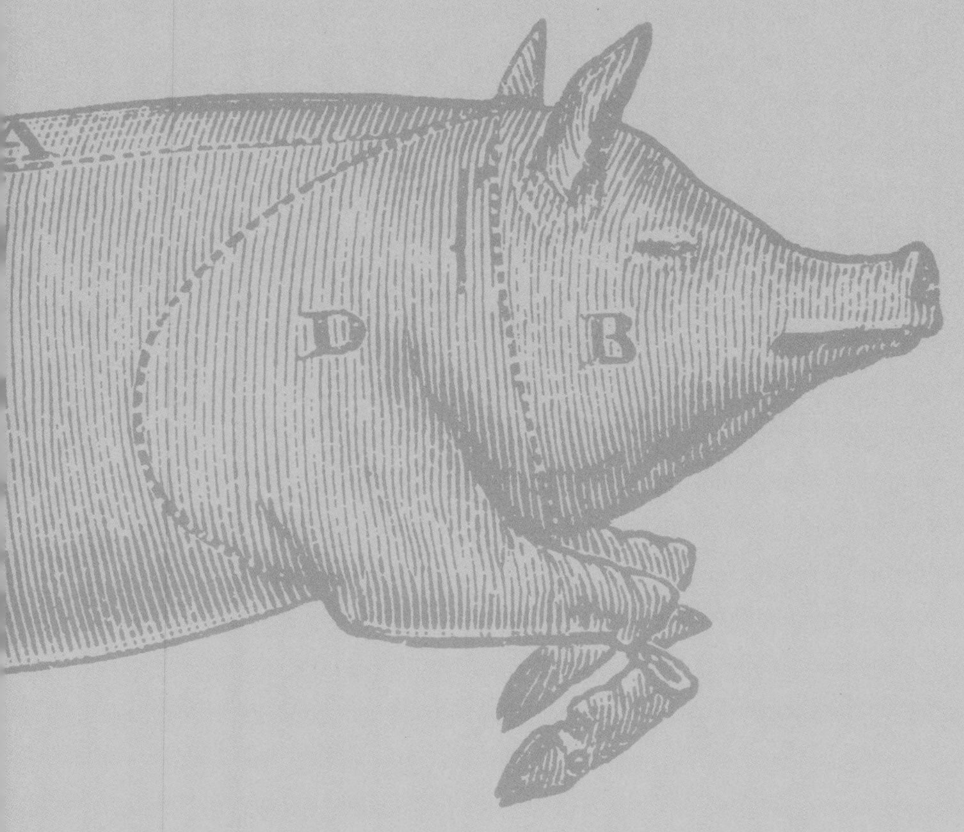

Overleaf The pork butcher's counter: chromolithograph from a manual of retail food display, Germany, *c.* 1912.

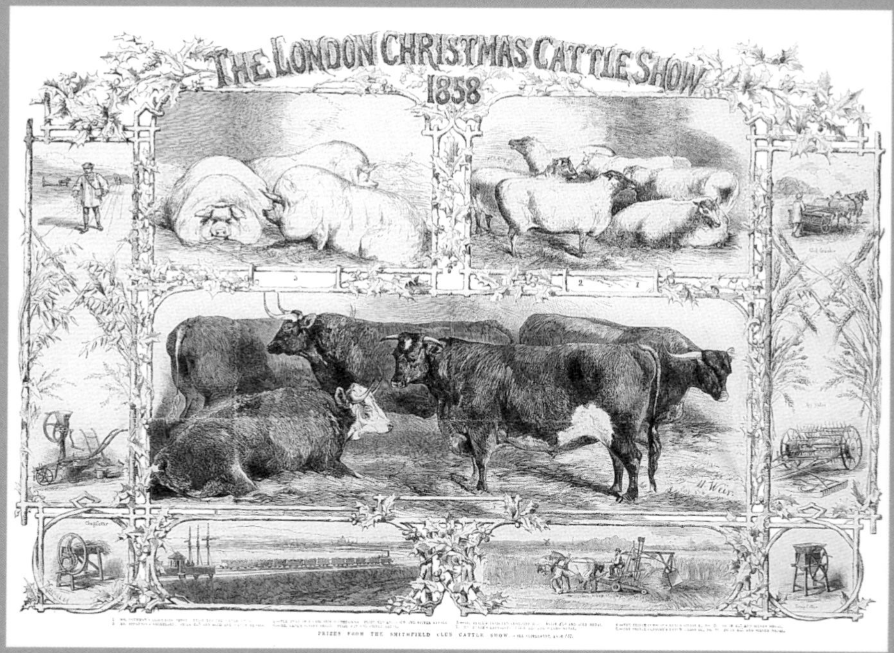

Above The London Christmas Cattle Show: wood engraving by H. Weir from *The Illustrated London News,* 1858.

Opposite The officials of a synagogue in East London seal the meat of orthodox Jews: illustration by P. Frenzeny from *The Illustrated London News,* 1903.

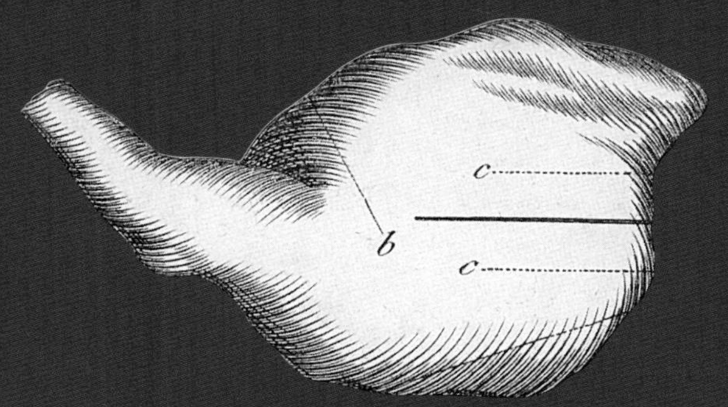

A SHOULDER of MUTTON No. 1.

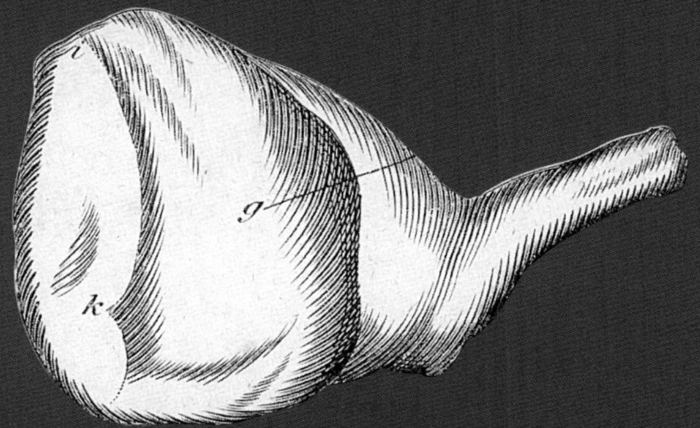

A SHOULDER of MUTTON No. 2.

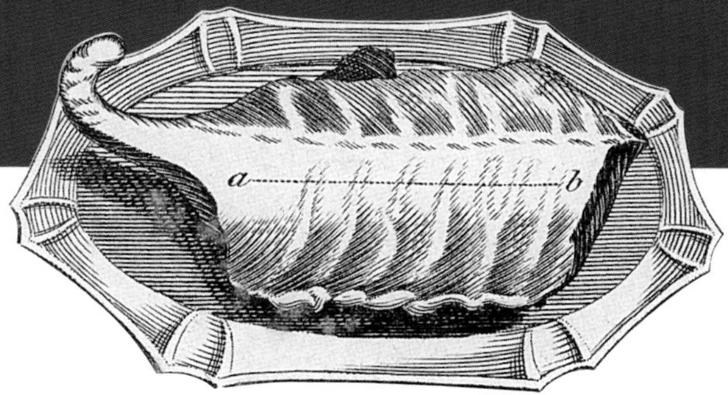

A SADDLE of MUTTON

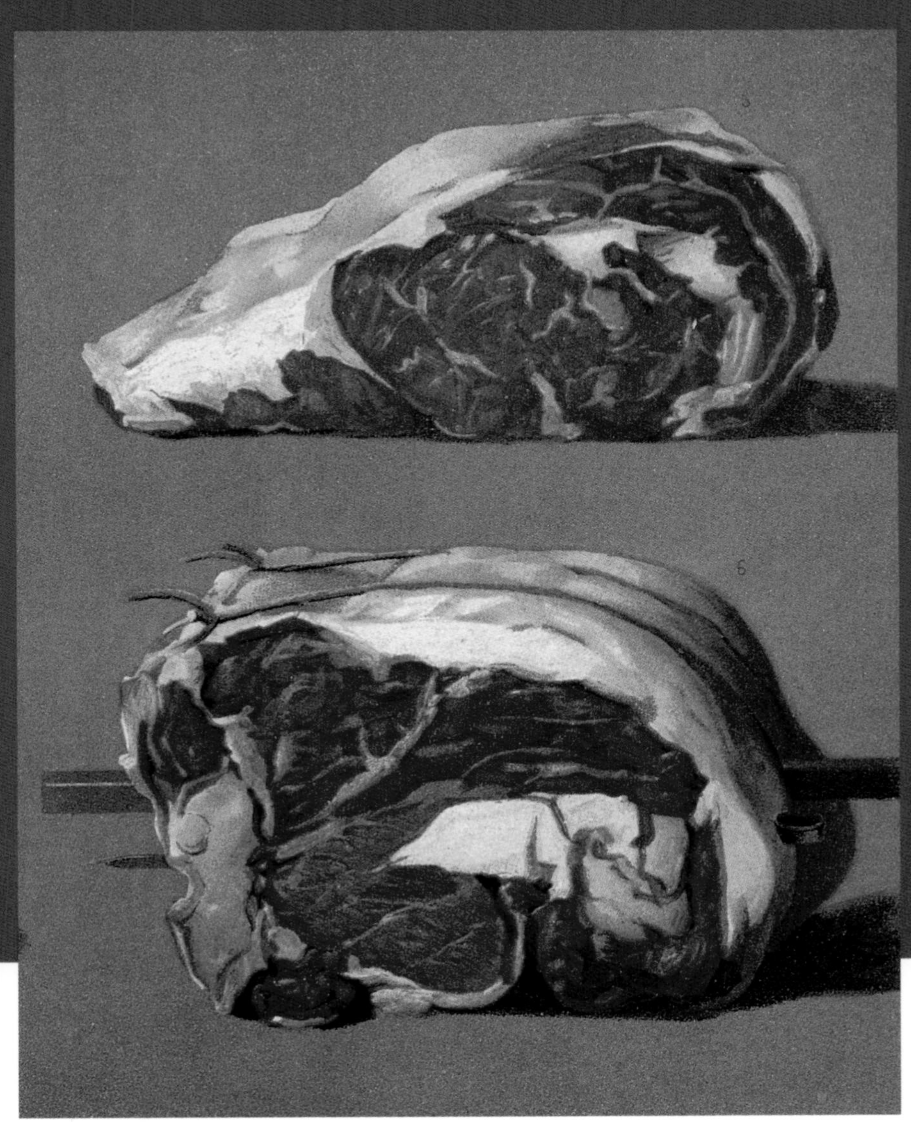

Opposite The art of carving mutton: copper engraving from *The Housekeeper's Instructor* by W. A. Henderson, London, 1793.

Above The *entrecôte* and *aloyau*: chromolithograph from *Le Livre de cuisine* by Jules Gouffé, Paris, 1867.

These pages Salting pork: copper engraving from Florinus' *Œconomus Prudens*, Nuremberg, 1702.

Opposite Preparing pheasant, hare and goose: copper engraving from *The Housekeeper's Instructor* by W. A. Henderson, London, 1793.

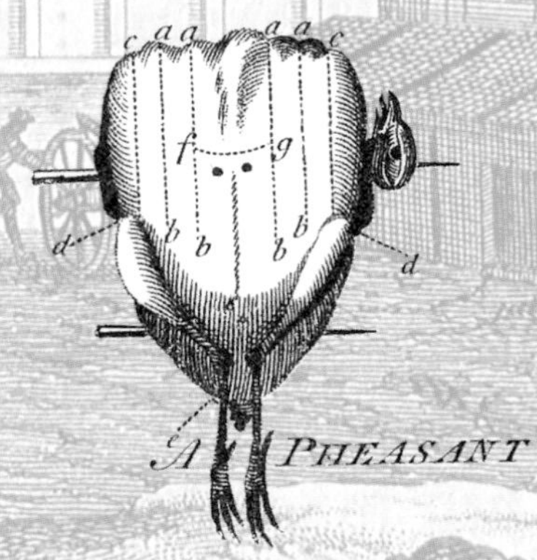

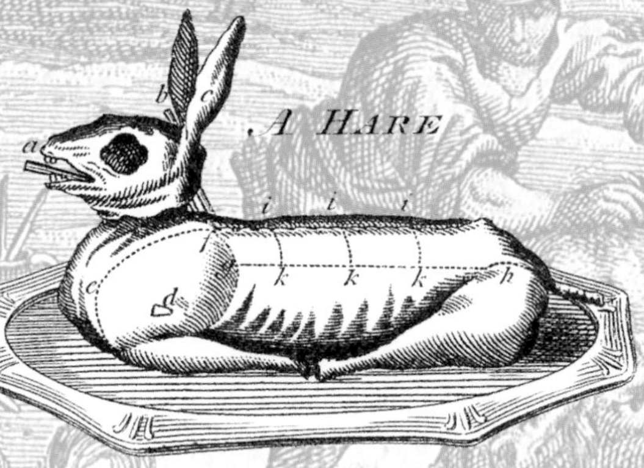

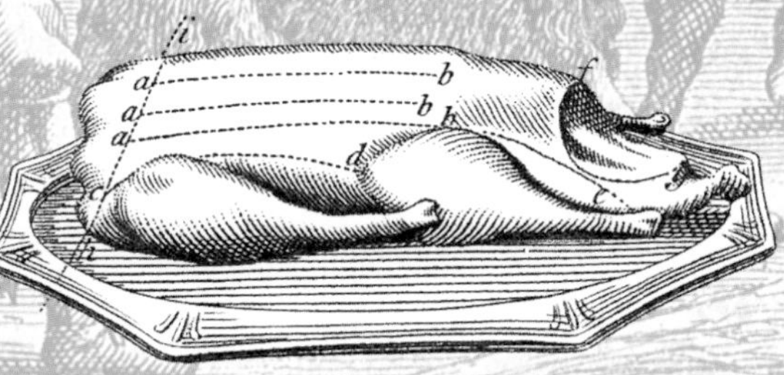

Rules for Carving.

This page Late nineteenth-century scenes in Parisian butchers' shops, including one specializing in horse-meat.

Opposite Example of mutton, including kidneys: chromolithograph from *Le Livre de cuisine* by Jules Gouffé, Paris, 1867.

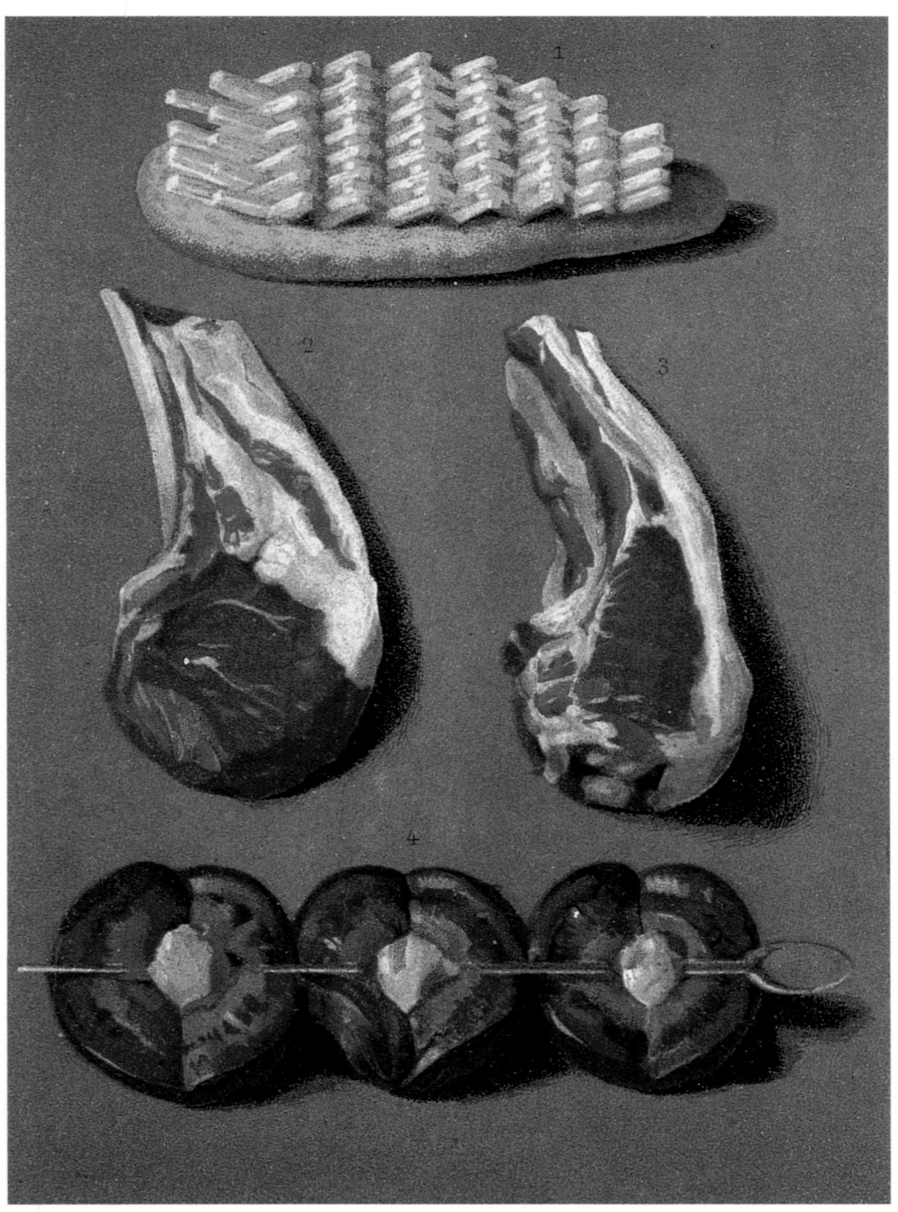

Overleaf The milking shed: copper engraving from Florinus' *Œconomus Přudens*, Nuremberg, 1702.

Above Butter-making: a colour card promoting the Liebig Meat Extract Company, *c.* 1912.

Opposite The little butter-makers: chromolithograph from *A Children's Book of Trades*, *c.* 1870.

HUDSON BROTHERS LUDGATE HILL. LONDON
PLANTS
Cheese Fair
Stilton
Aylesbury Dairy Compy:
Cheese-Making
Cutting up Curd in the Vat
The Curd Mill:
filling the Vats
The Cheese Press.
AYLESBURY DAIRY Co
Butter
Churning
Making up the Butter

Left Cheese manufacture, using automatic stirrers: anonymous wood engravings, *c.* 1880.

Opposite Cheese- and butter-making, and prize cheeses at the dairy show – demonstrations by employees of the Aylesbury Dairy Company: wood engraving from *The Illustrated London News*, 1876.

EXTRAIT DE VIANDE DE LA C^IE LIEBIG
J. v. Liebig
LE FROMAGE — Hollande.
Tournage et coloriage du fromage d'Edam.
Reproduction interdite.
Voir l'explication au verso.

Left and *below* Cheese-making illustrated on Liebig cards, *c.* 1912.

LIBOX, EXTRAIT DE VIANDE ASSAISONNÉ
LIBOX
LE FROMAGE — Suisse.
Le pesage sur un alpage.
Reproduction interdite.
Voir l'explication au verso.

Opposite Bee-keeping and the manufacture of artificial honeycombs: series of illustrations from *The Pictorial World*, 1883.

2
3
5
HOGE'S
HIVE
HIVE
HIVE
6
8
9

Above The baker: copper engraving from Florinus' *Œconomus Prudens*, Nuremberg, 1702.

Right The home baker: late nineteenth-century French wood engraving.

Opposite The *boulanger*: coloured woodcut, Paris, *c.* 1860.

Above The great French ginger-bread maker takes a new batch of kings out of the oven: political caricature by James Gillray, *c.* 1810.

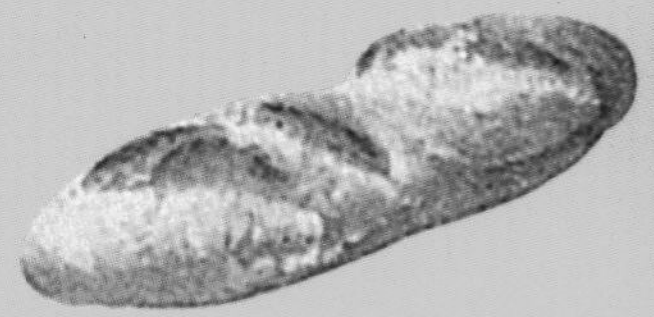

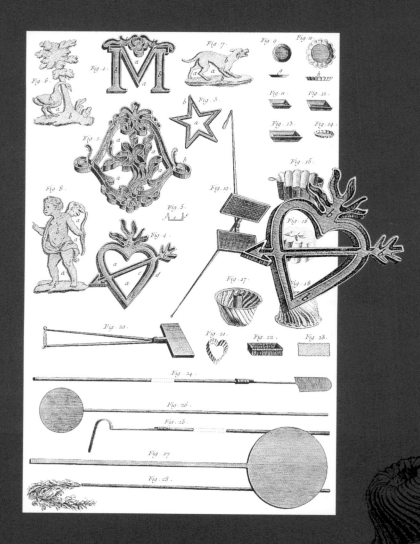

Above The confectioner's and pastry-cook's utensils: copper engraving, Paris, *c.* 1780.

Above A Dutch pie-maker and his apprentice: woodcut by Jan Luyken, *c.* 1745.

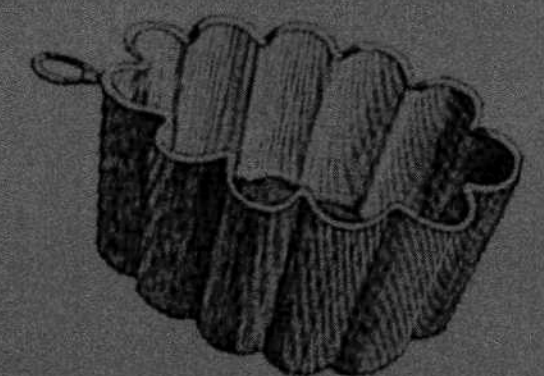

Above The little bakers: colour illustration from *A Children's Book of Trades*, *c.* 1870.

Opposite French bread: chromolithograph, Paris, *c.* 1900.

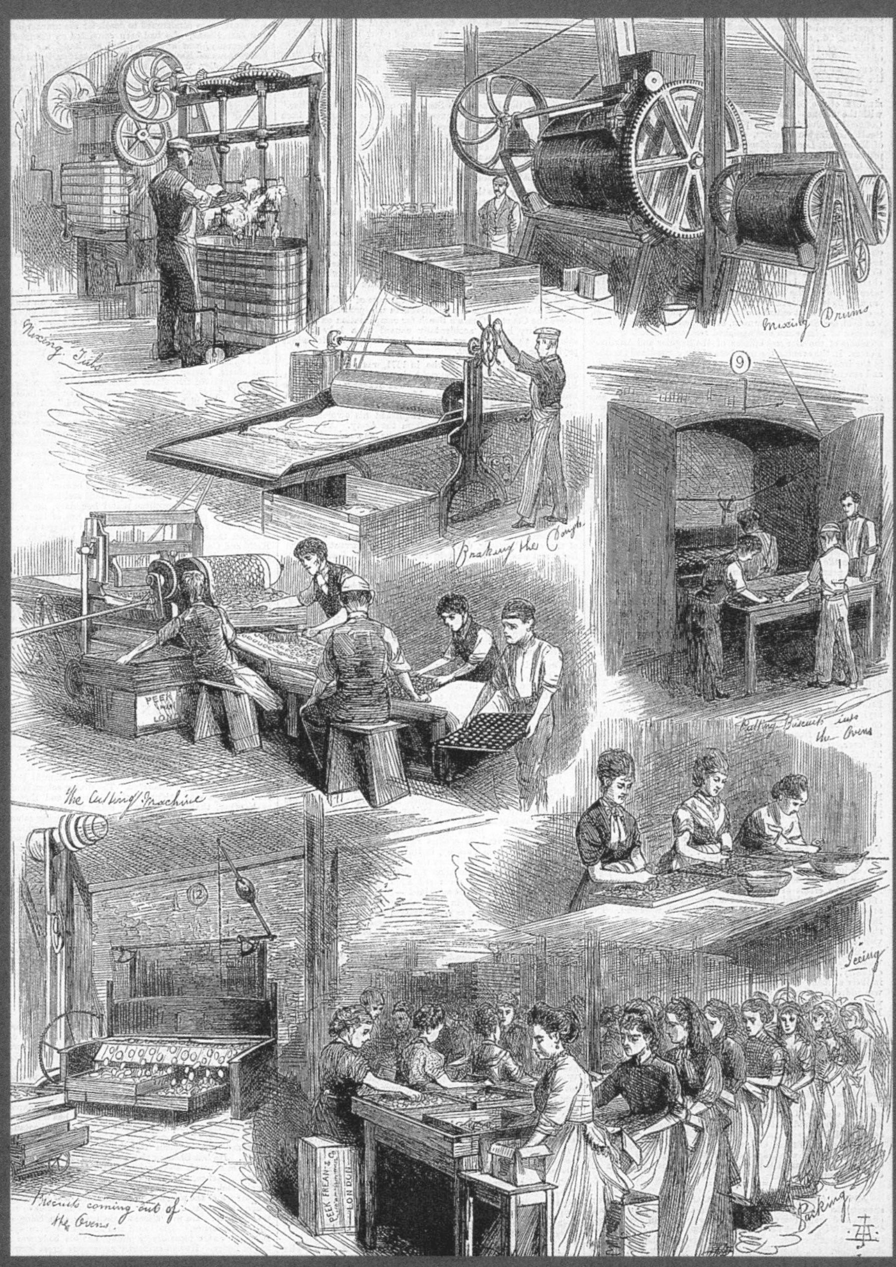
Mixing Tub
Mixing Drums
Braking the Dough
Putting Biscuits into the Ovens
The Cutting Machine
Icing
Biscuits coming out of the Ovens
PEEK FREAN & Co LONDON
Packing

Opposite The biscuit factory: wood engraving from *The Illustrated London News*, 1874.

Below The gingerbread-makers: woodcut by Jan Luyken, *c.* 1742.

Above Life in Naples, including a *pizzeria*: wood engraving from *The Graphic*, 1881.

Opposite A Parisian baker at work: illustration from *The Illustrated London News*, 1906.

Left The baker at work: finely etched copper plate by Johann-Christoph Weigel, Germany, *c.* 1700.

Below The pieman and his wares: steel engraving by J. Moore, *c.* 1840.

Opposite The pancake woman: anonymous mezzotint printed for Carrington Bowles, London, *c.* 1780.

Overleaf In the confectioner's kitchen; copper engraving from *The New Royal Universal Dictionary of Arts and Sciences*, London, *c.* 1780.

Fig. 1.
Fig. 2.

Fig. 3.
Fig. 1.

Opposite Collecting and sorting raw sugar cane, grinding, boiling and testing the juice: wood engraving from *The Graphic*, 1876.

Above Rice mortars and wheat and cotton-seed hullers: illustrations from *The Growth of Industrial Art,* Washington, 1892.

Overleaf Processing equipment for the small farm: steel engraving by F. A. Brockhaus, Leipzig, *c.* 1850.

17
12
24
2
3
18
4
13
14
9

22
23
15
6
5
16
7
11
19

Above Cocoa mill on Grenada, West Indies: wood engraving from *The Illustrated London News*, 1855.

Opposite Preparing cinnamon: copper engraving, *c.* 1780.

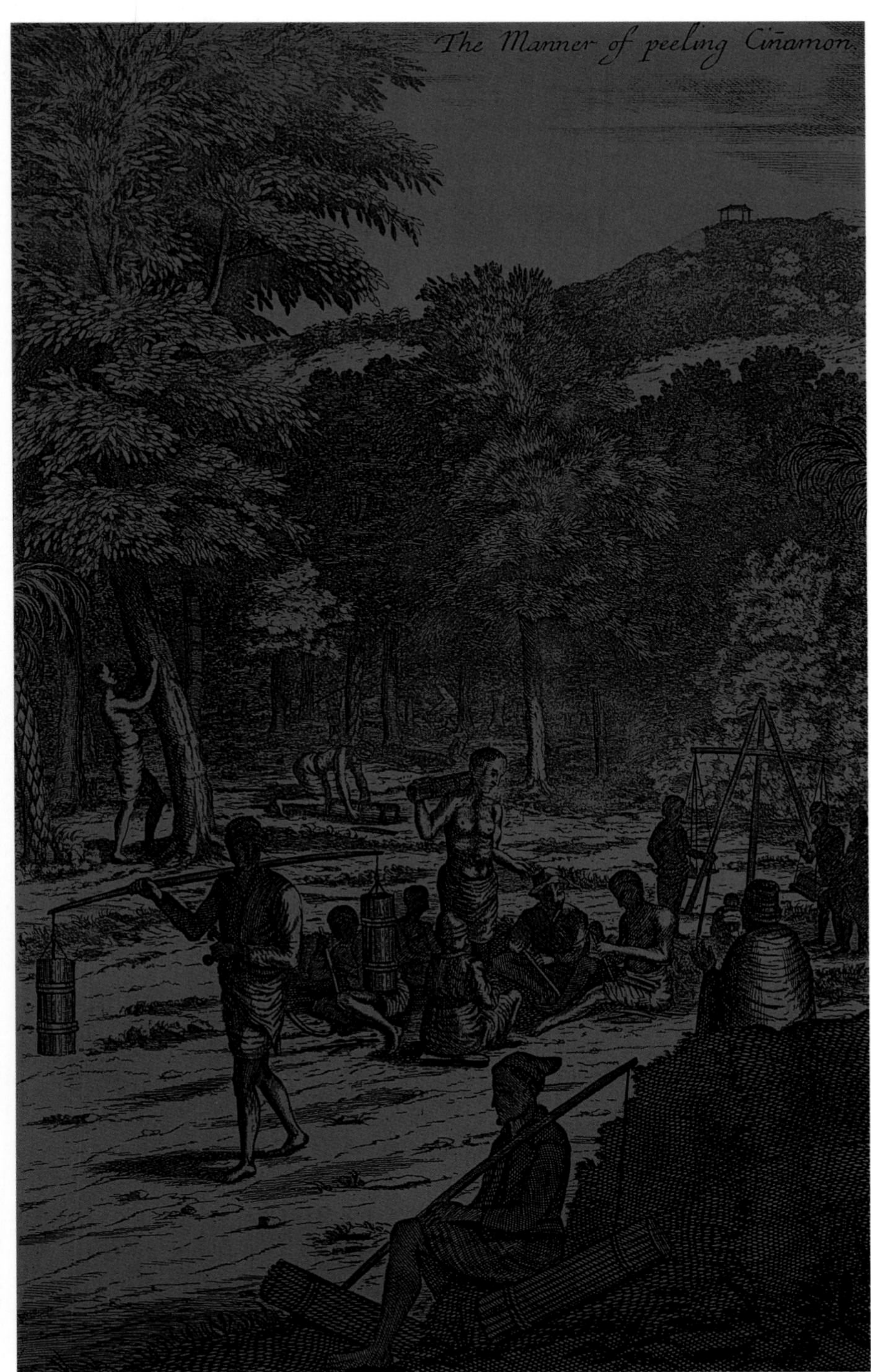
The Manner of peeling Ciñamon.

AT THE OFFICE.

CARRYING TEA-CHESTS TO THE SHIP.

TEA IN BED.

WEIGHING TEA-CHESTS.

ON BOARD SHIP.

Above Varieties of distillery: illustrations from *The Growth of Industrial Art*, Washington, 1892.

Left and *below* Varieties of French drinking: wine-tasting in seventeenth-century Burgundy; cider-making in Normandy in the late nineteenth century.

—3—

The Still-lifes of the Larder

And more from Cupboard and Kitchen Garden

The concept of the larder may seem somewhat anachronistic; produce now normally makes its way to the table via the refrigerator and cooker, both of which are probably installed in the kitchen. Yet, how important in the past has this interim staging-post been, whether for harbouring the longer-term results of home-preserving or as a preparation place for the more immediately consumable produce of market and kitchen garden.

Some of the most impressive imagery of the contents of the larder, we noted, appears in the work of seventeenth-century Dutch and Flemish painters, often seen in the form of engravings and mezzotints after their works. One particularly memorable work is the large coloured mezzotint (page 177) by the English engraver, Richard Earlom, after a painting by Martin de Vos, showing a cook selecting a hare from a colossal display of just about everything the ideal larder should contain – a super-abundance of game and exotic fruits.

Opposite The contents of the larder: copper engraving, Germany, early eighteenth century.

There are certain conventions in the display of food and drink in these still-lifes: vessels and dishes set out upon a table top, usually with some hint of disorder or indication of recent consumption, but no sitters at the table; it really looks as though the prime contents of the larder have been, literally, tipped out on to the table to form an exquisite composition of game, bread, cheese and fruit. In the latter part of the seventeenth century, the Dutch painters began to work in the 'sumptuous' fashion, piling succulent foods of all kinds high in a setting of glorious table coverings and fine tableware.

The idea of plenty in the larder is frequently accompanied by the notion of ill-doing, of the theft of especially desirable foods; and from time to time in these pages we come across images of unwelcome visits from predators to larder and kitchen. In Victorian England, though in cruder form, the still-life of gastronomic plenty seems to have enjoyed resurgent popularity. Many such paintings were reproduced as special plates in popular reviews, most notably in *The Illustrated London News.*

The great Brillat-Savarin devoted one of his most evocative meditations to the subject of fowls in the larder – *nos garde-mangers*, a term which simply conveys the pre-kitchen nature of the larder. His prose is lyrical in its eulogies of quail, woodcock and pheasant, although the latter, it is claimed, ranks behind the partridge and the chicken if foolishly consumed within a week of death. His praise of the turkey, the *coq d'Inde*, will undoubtedly attract the approbation of Anglo-Saxon gourmands, but his inclusive attitude to game birds is entirely French. His first category begins with the thrush, then in descending order, those of lesser volume, including the robin, warbler and ortolan.

Most of the images in this chapter, then, are drawn from representations of foodstuffs just prior to preparation for the kitchen or even of the process of preparation. And close to the well-stocked larder would have been the well-run kitchen garden, the *potager*. As further decoration to these pages, then, we have included some images of its fruits to counterbalance the images of game and meats. Fruit and vegetables, after all, do introduce a gentler note – tending rather than slaughtering.

These pages Details of endive and artichoke from a mid-nineteenth-century series of prints.

1 *Cinara maxima Anglica.*
The great red Artichoke.

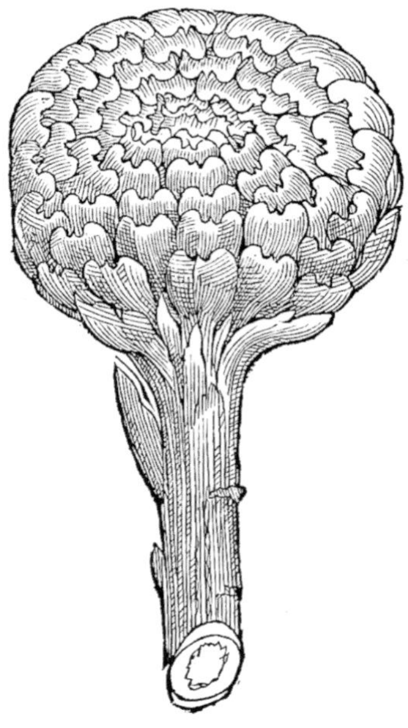

2 *Cinara maxima alba.*
The great white Artichoke.

3 *Cinara sylvestris.*
Wilde Artichoke.

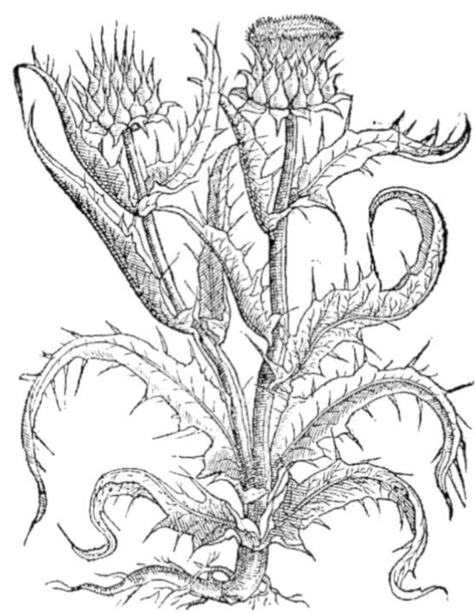

These pages Artichokes, garlic, onions and ginger from *The Herball or General Historie of Plantes* by John Gerarde, London, 1597.

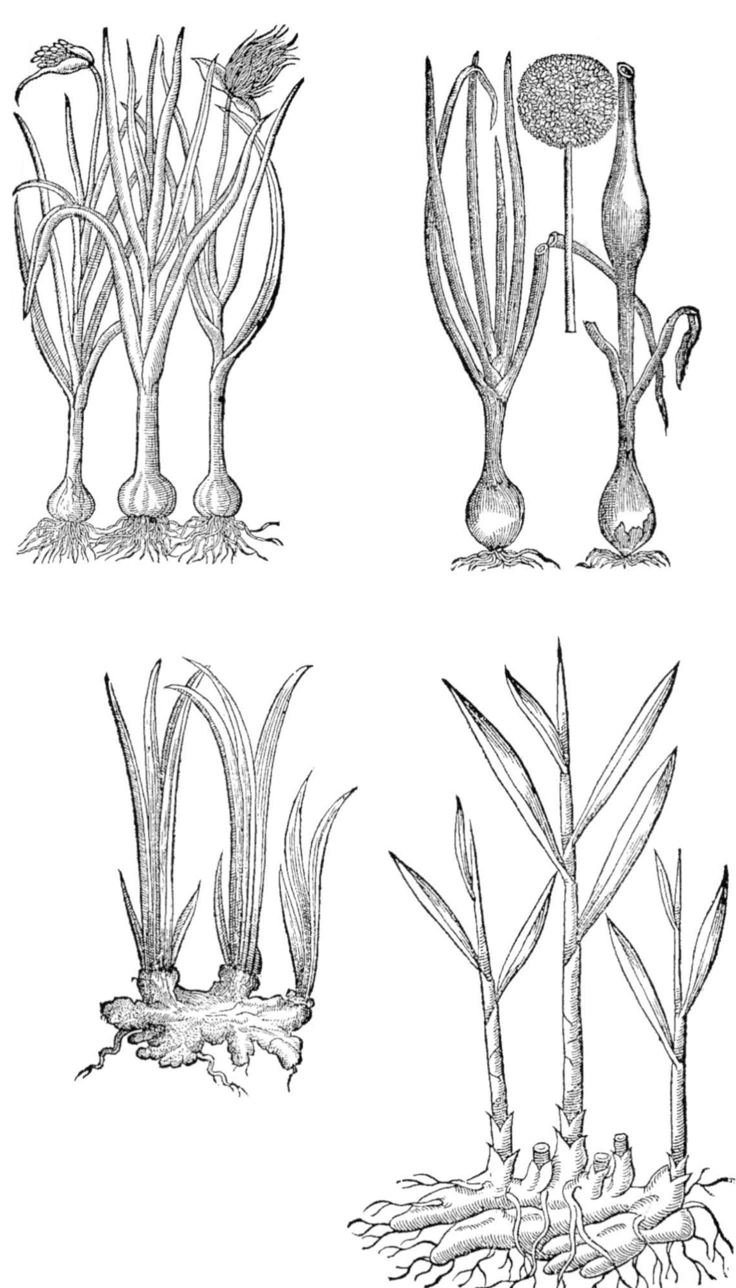

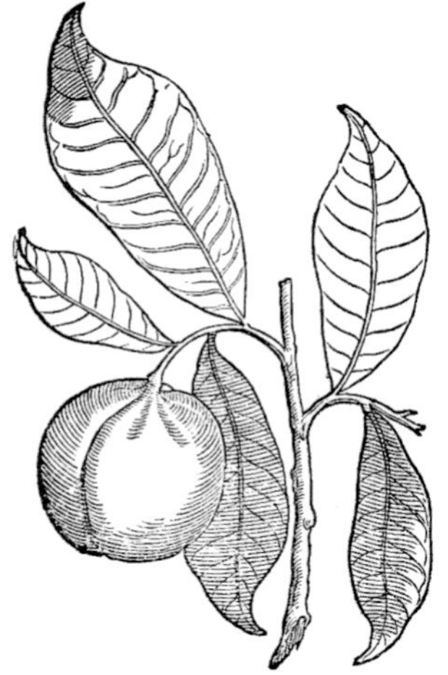

These pages More illustrations from Gerarde's *Herball (clockwise for each page)*: nutmeg, pepper, parsley, mint, common fennel and dill.

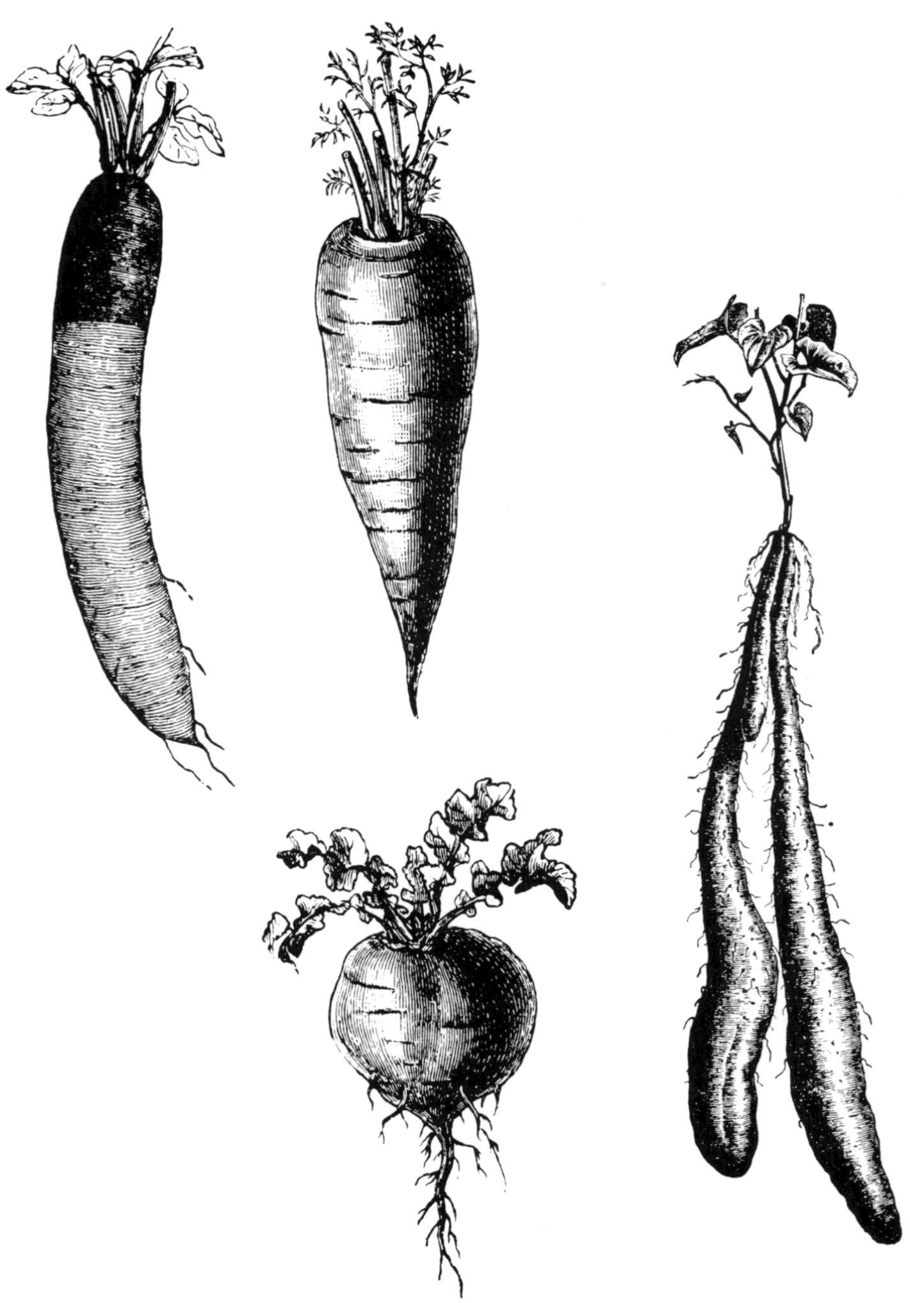

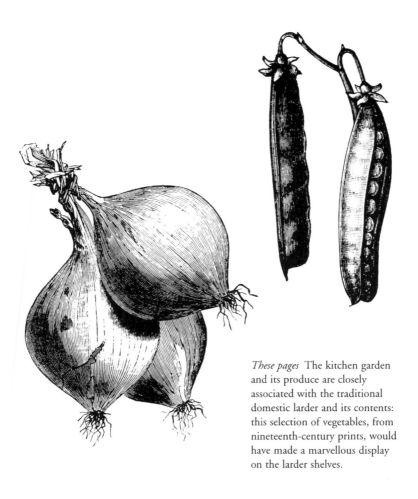

These pages The kitchen garden and its produce are closely associated with the traditional domestic larder and its contents: this selection of vegetables, from nineteenth-century prints, would have made a marvellous display on the larder shelves.

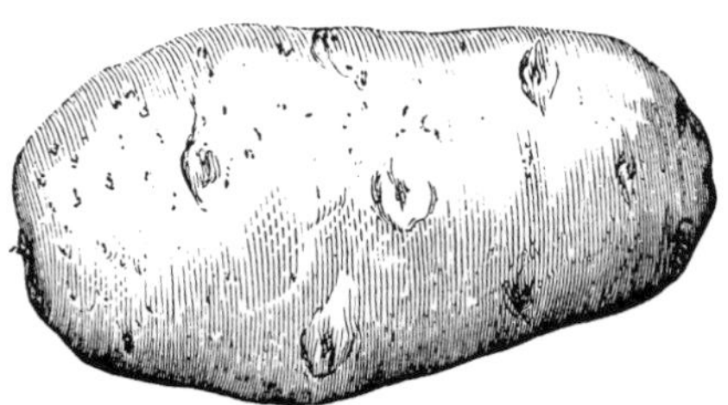

12
11
10
9
8
7

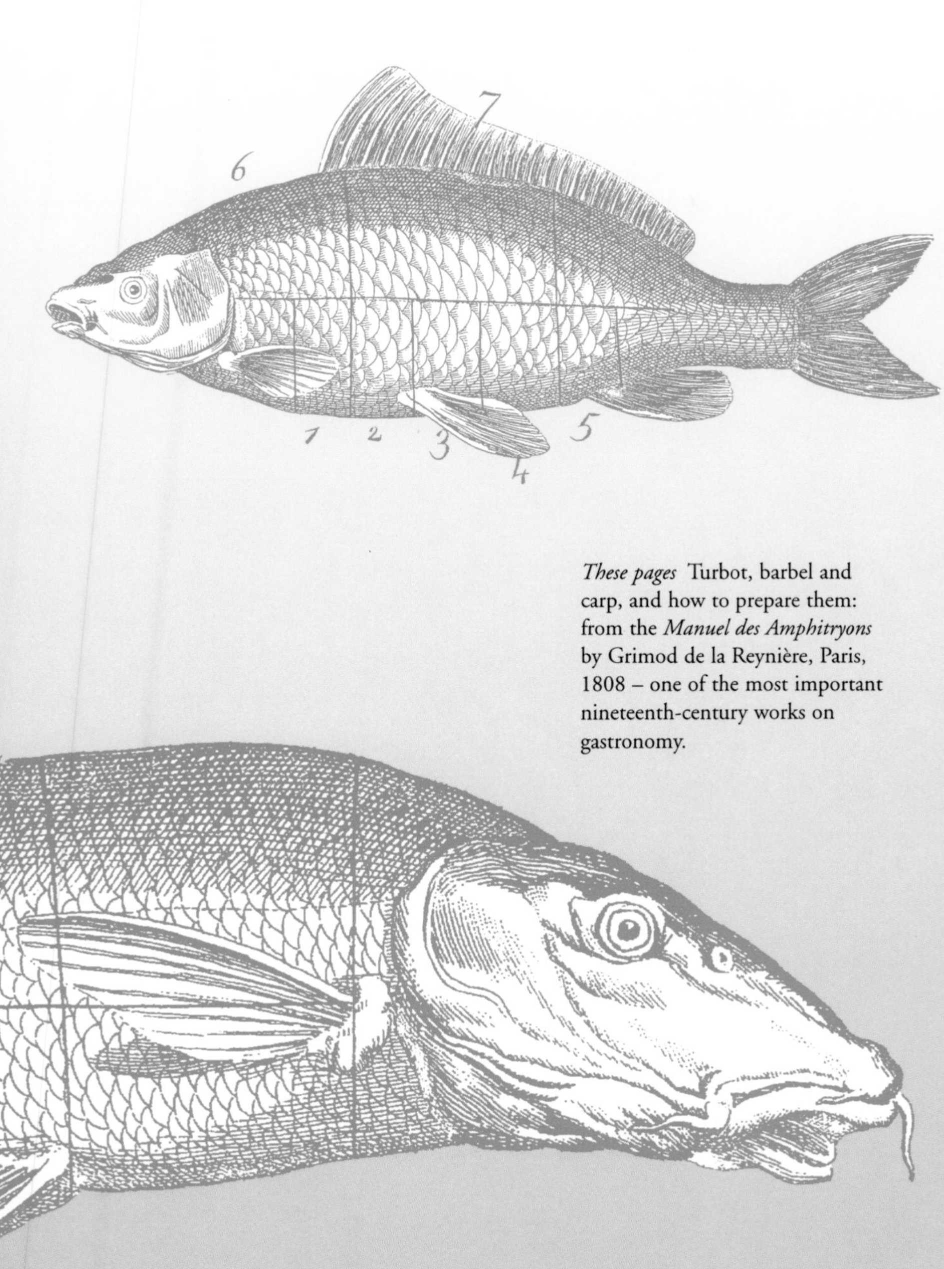

These pages Turbot, barbel and carp, and how to prepare them: from the *Manuel des Amphitryons* by Grimod de la Reynière, Paris, 1808 – one of the most important nineteenth-century works on gastronomy.

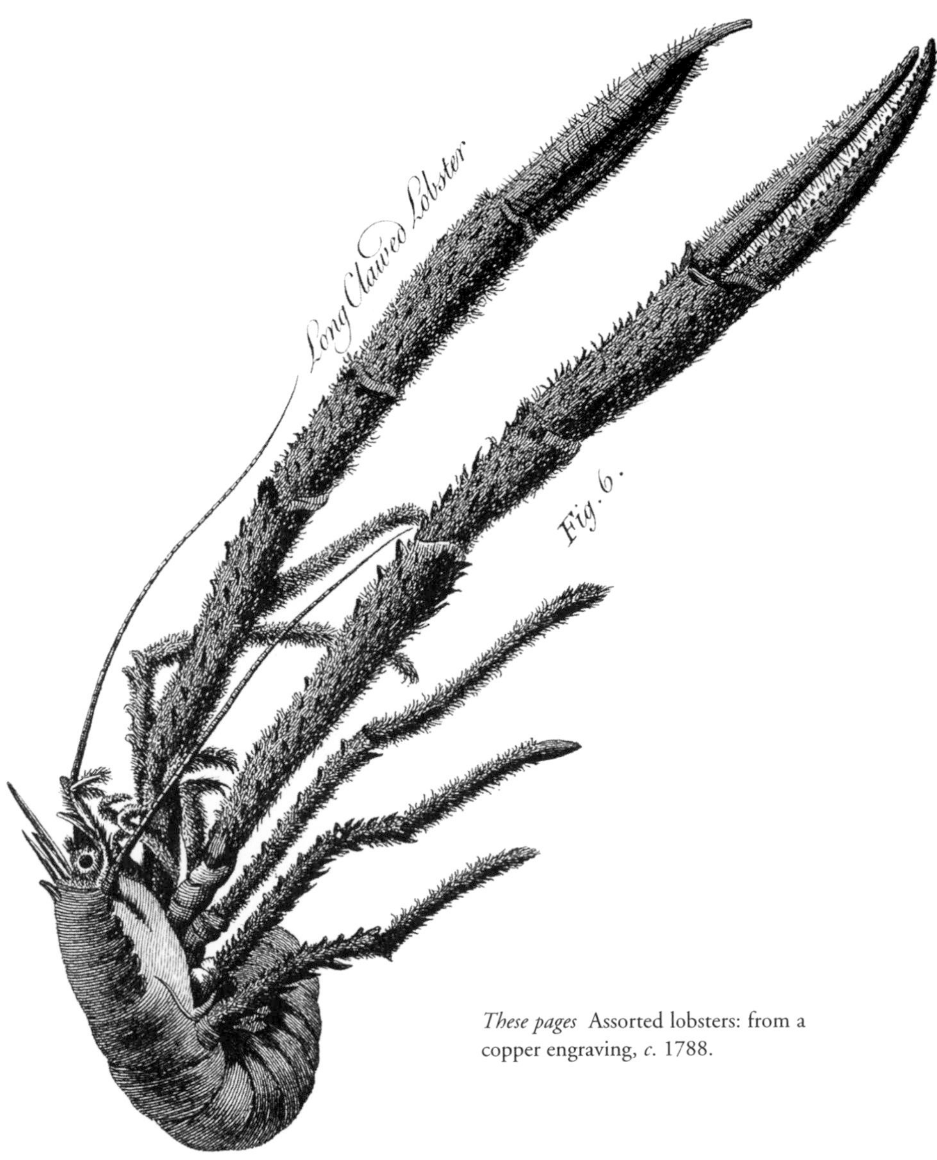

These pages Assorted lobsters: from a copper engraving, *c.* 1788.

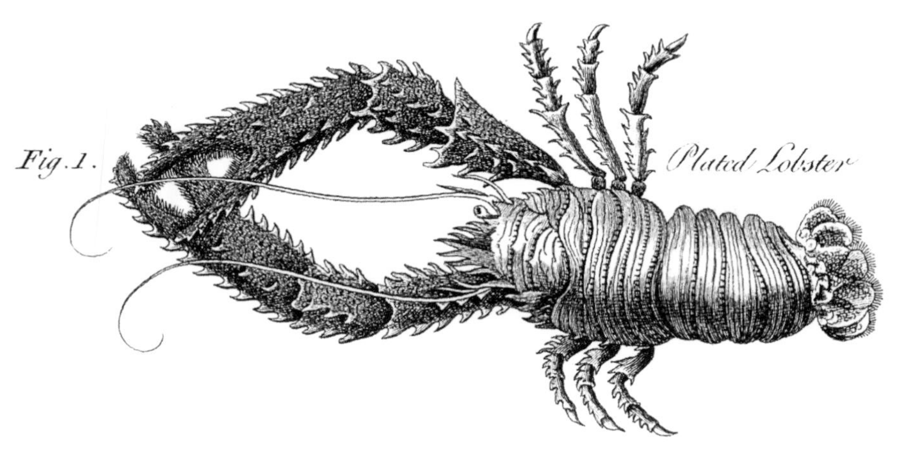
Fig. 1.
Plated Lobster

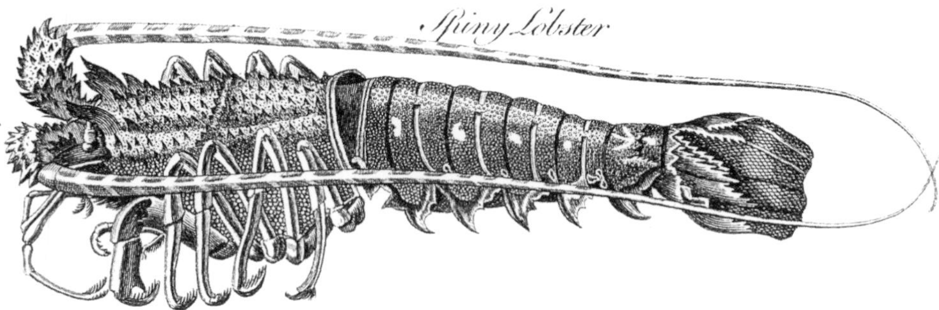
Spiny Lobster
Fig. 2.

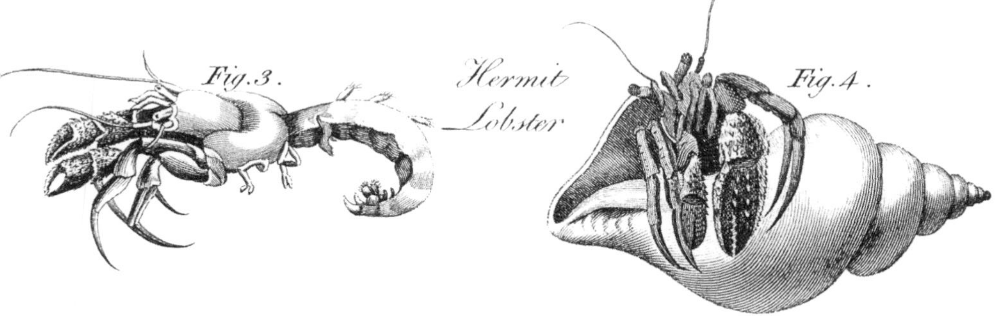
Fig. 3.
Hermit Lobster
Fig. 4.

Norway Lobster
Fig. 5.

I
H
G
E
F
D
C
B
A
A
B
D
E
C

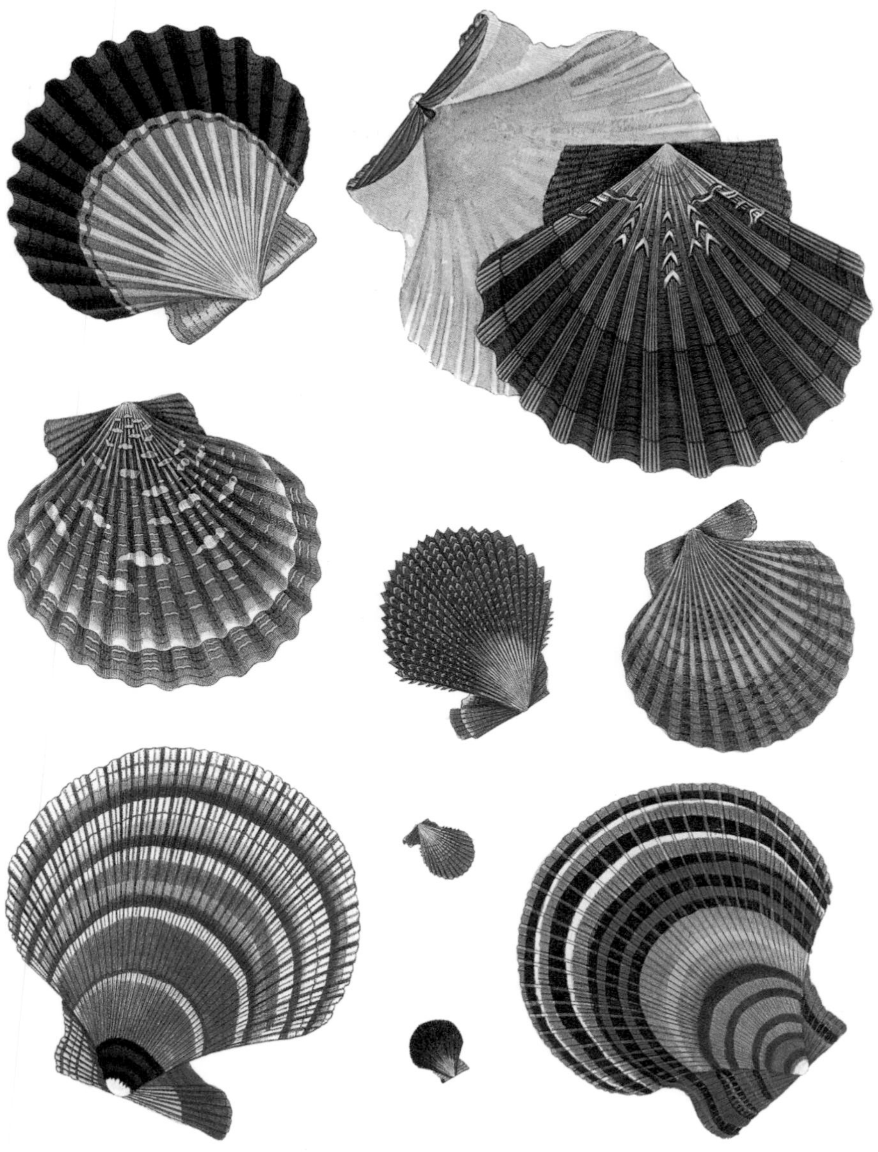

Opposite Fish and crustaceans from Sri Lanka and Indonesia: copper engraving, *c.* 1710.

Above Ostrea (shells), a selection of scallops: hand-coloured copper engraving from J. Wilkes' *London Encyclopedia*, 1810.

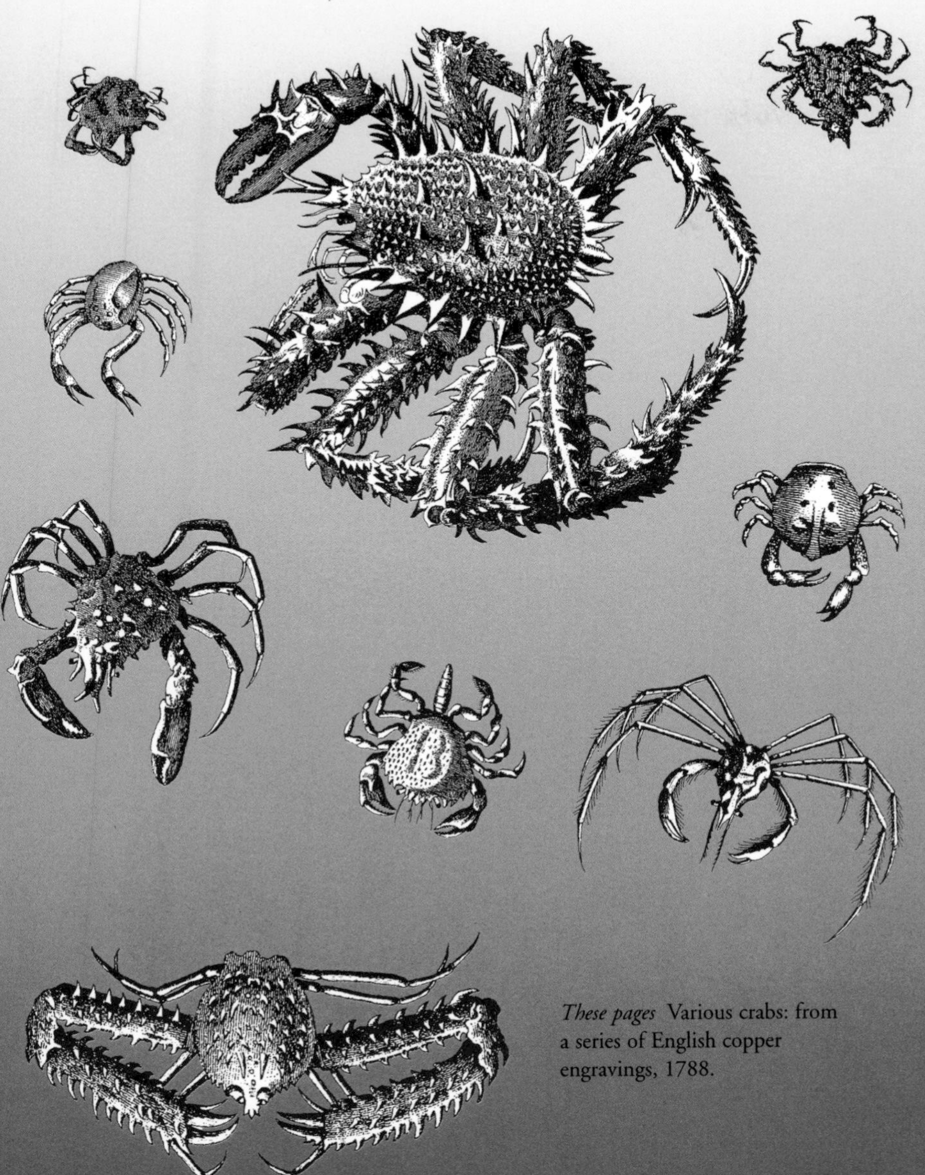

These pages Various crabs: from a series of English copper engravings, 1788.

m
c
o
n
m
e
a

These pages Wonders of the sea, including turtle, crab, lobster, octopus and trout: chromolithograph, Germany, *c*. 1880.

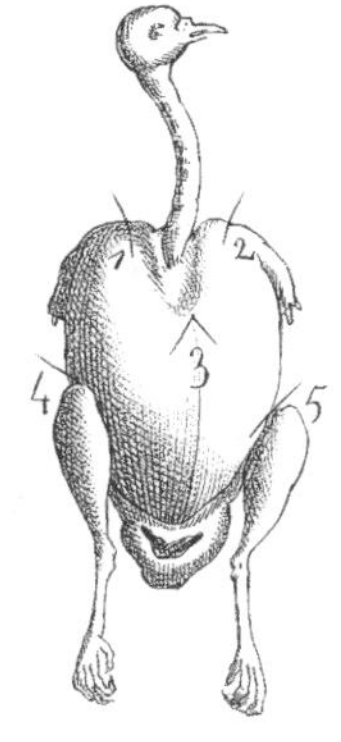

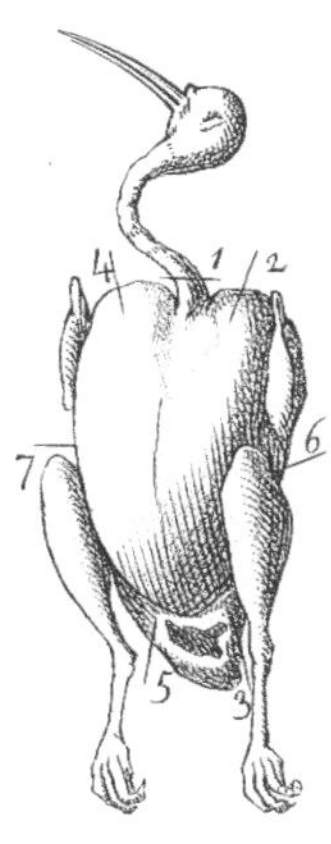

Above Preparing fowl: from Grimod de la Reynière's *Manuel des Amphitryons*, 1808.

Left Dead swan, game and fruit: engraving by J. Williamson after W. Duffield from *The Illustrated London News*, 1860.

Overleaf Poultry prepared for the kitchen: chromolithograph from Jules Gouffé's *Le Livre de cuisine*, Paris, 1867.

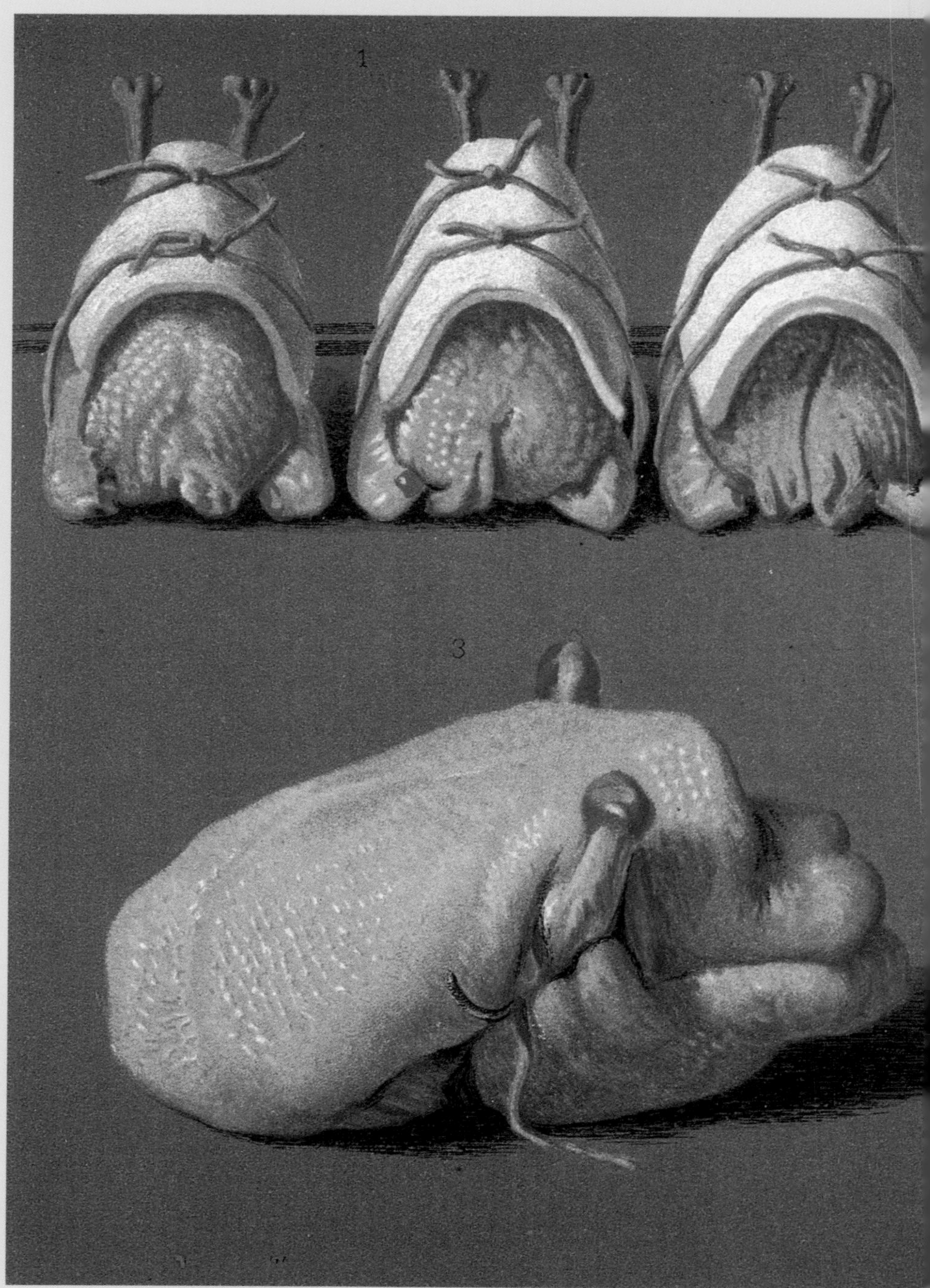
1
3

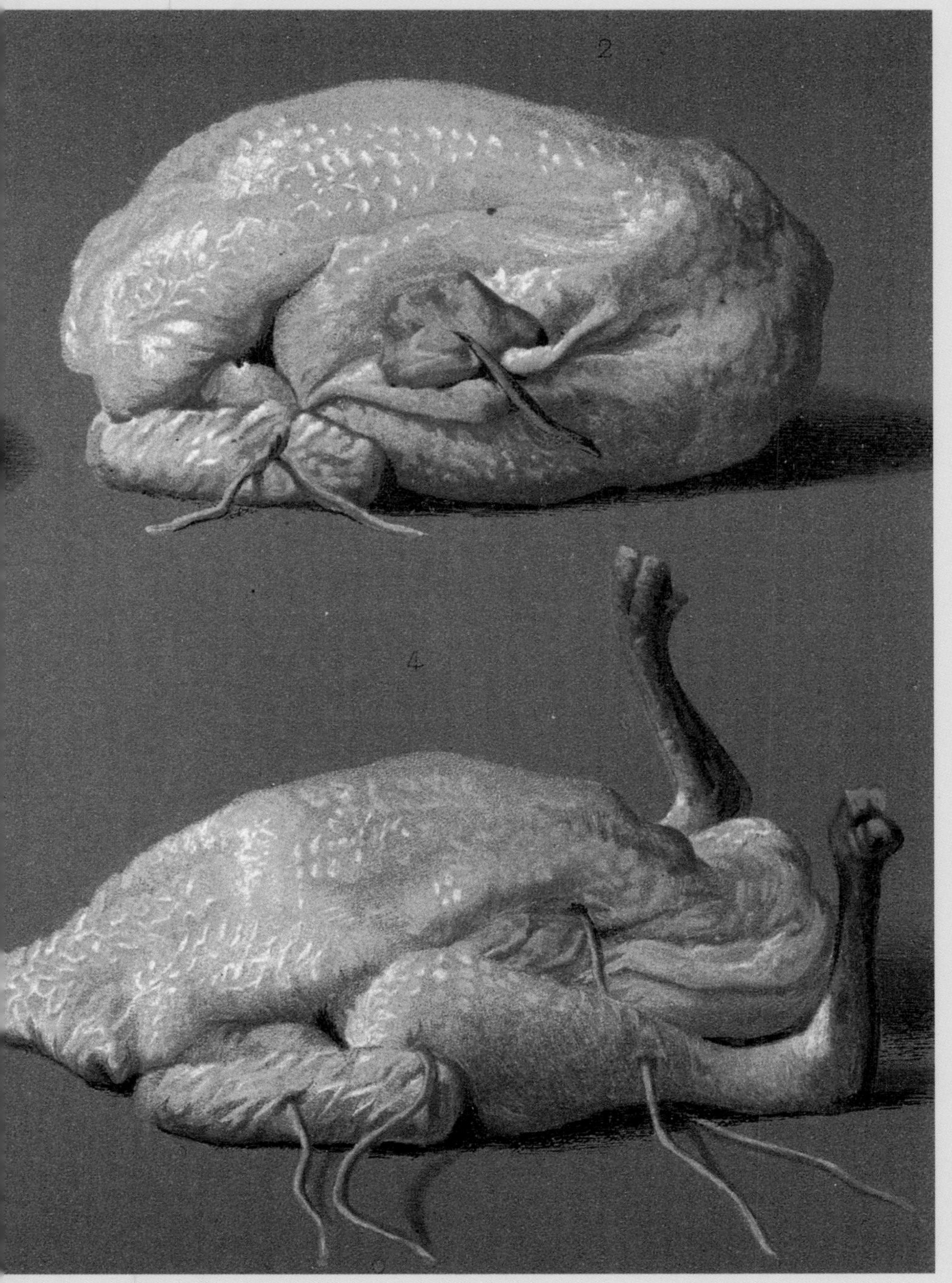
2
4

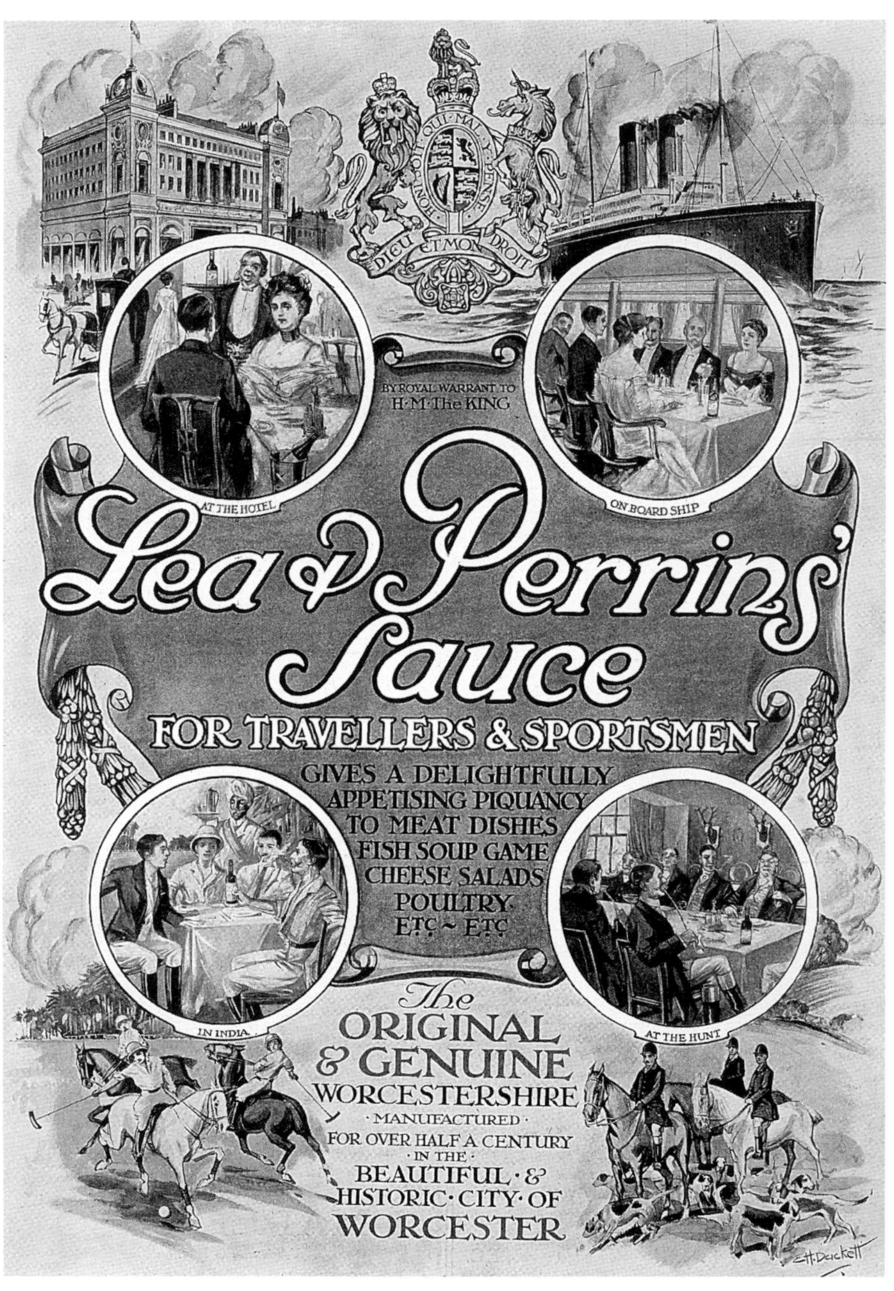

Above Lea & Perrin's famous Worcester Sauce: advertisement from *The Illustrated London News*, 1903.

Above 'How perfect everything is here!': advertisement for Colman's Mustard from *The Illustrated London News, c.* 1890, associating it with the luxury of the liner *Mauretania.*

Above Christmas presents – a display of seasonal game: chromolithograph after a painting by William Duffield, 1859.

Below 'Poularde à la Godard': chromolithograph from *Le Livre de cuisine* by Jules Gouffé, Paris, 1867.

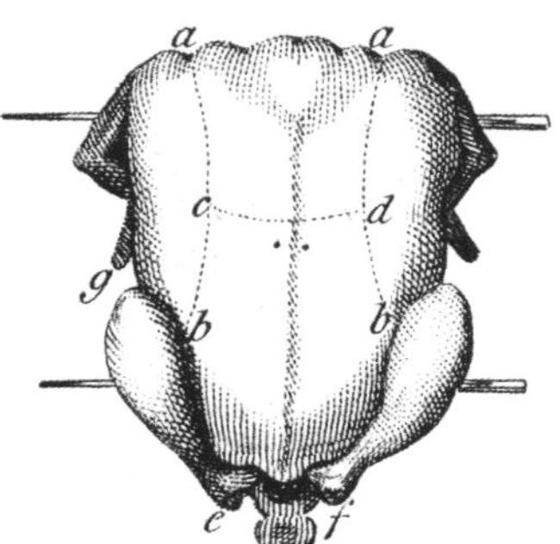

BOIL'D FOWL

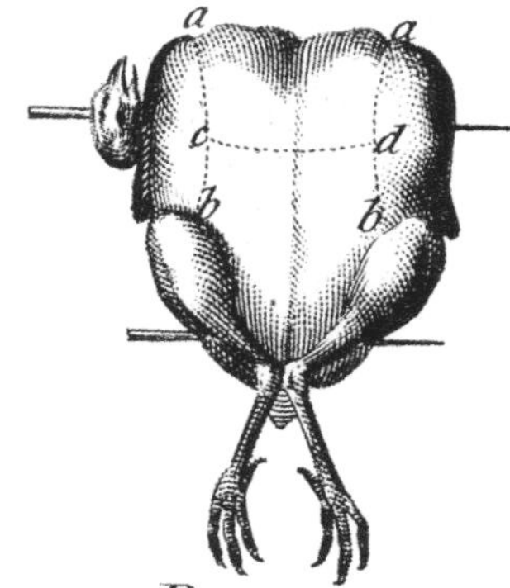

PARTRIDGE

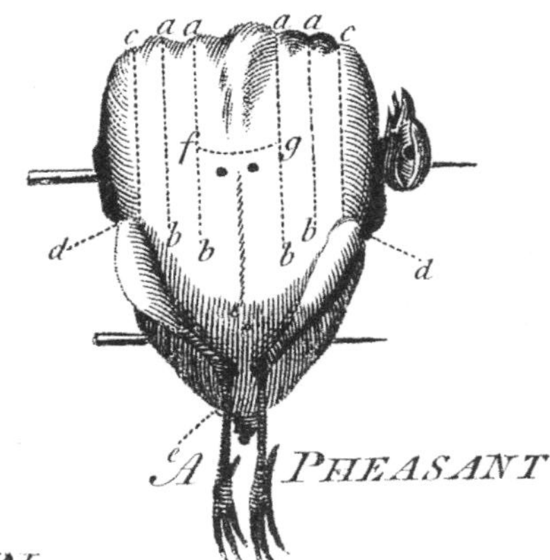

A PHEASANT

PIGEON

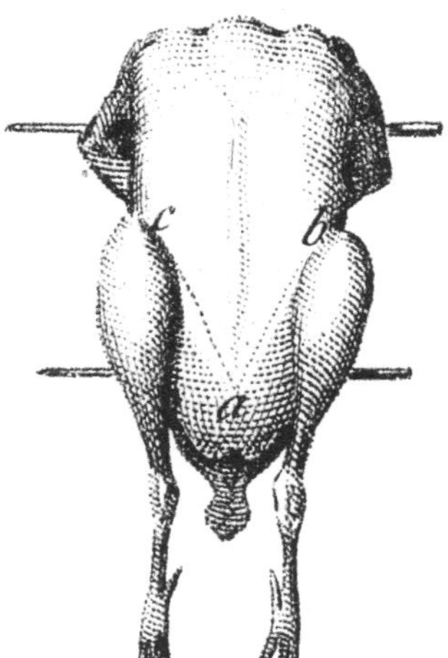

PIGEON

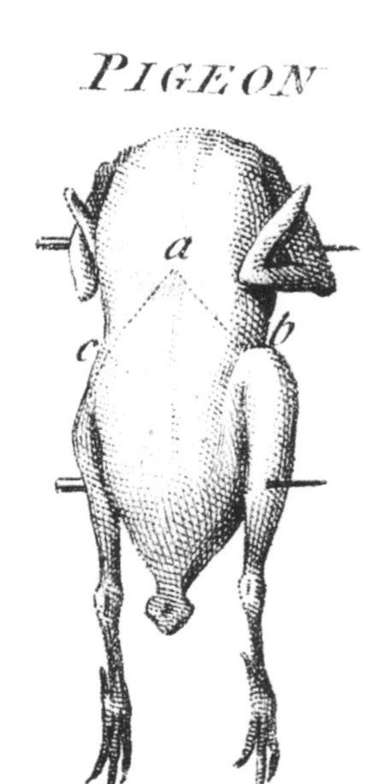

a clean cloth to remove the skins, then pound them till quite a smooth paste with three ounces of castor sugar, and a few drops of Marshall's carmine, mix this with four raw yolks of eggs, and add to it by degrees half a pint of single cream, and stir in a stewpan over the fire till the mixture thickens, then add a wineglass of Marshall's maraschino syrup, and a wineglass of Silver Rays (white) rum, rub through a tammy with spoons, getting as much of the almond mixture through as possible, put it into the bain marie to get hot before using, or it may be served cold.

Aubois Sauce.—Put half a pound of lump sugar with half a pint of water, and boil until a little of the sugar taken between the wetted finger and thumb forms a thread without breaking when the fingers are opened, and then pour it on to five raw yolks of eggs and whip till quite cold; put it on ice, and before using add half a pint of whipped cream, and flavour it with maraschino, Silver Rays (white) rum, or other liqueur; keep on ice till required.

Apricot or Jam Sauce.—Half a pot of apricot or any other jam, two tablespoonfuls of castor sugar, four tablespoonfuls of water; boil for ten minutes, then pass it all through a tammy or sieve. Add a little carmine and a wineglassful of Silver Rays (white) rum and a wineglass of maraschino or noyeau syrup.

Chocolate Sauce.—Put into a stewpan half a pint of water, three ounces of Marshall's icing sugar, and three ounces of Fry's vanilla chocolate cut up; bring to the boil, and when it has dissolved mix into it one ounce of crême de riz that has been mixed with two tablespoonfuls of cold water and coloured with a little of Marshall's coffee brown; boil together for about five minutes, then tammy and use. This is also good served cold.

Coffee Sauce.—To serve hot or cold with puddings, sweets le from light cakes, and cold soufflés.—Put six good spoonfuls of ground Mocha coffee into a cafetière and over it three gills of boiling water; let it remain in the arie until all has run through the pot, then strain on e ounces of castor sugar and five raw yolks of eggs e been mixed up together in a basin, put the mixture a clean stewpan, dissolve in it two sheets of gelatine, and stir it in the bain marie until it

thickens to the consistency of thick cream, then rub it thro the tammy, make hot in the bain marie and use. If sauce is served cold, one gill of stiffly whipped cream sho be added when about to be served.

Orange Flower Water Sauce.—To serve with hot or col soufflés, puddings, &c.—Put into a stewpan eight raw yolks of eggs, three tablespoonfuls of orange flower water, three ounces of castor sugar, three tablespoonfuls of thick cream, and a saltspoonful of essence of vanilla, stir these all together until it comes to the thickness of cream, standing the stewpan in the bain marie; when thick rub it through the tammy. It may be poured round the sweet and sprinkled with crystallised rose leaves, or served in a boat with the leaves lightly sprinkled on the top.

Pistachio or Maraschino Sauce.—To serve with hot puddings, ices, soufflés, &c.—Put a quarter of a pound of pistachio kernels into cold water, and bring them to the boil, rub them in a cloth to remove the skins, pound them in the mortar till perfectly smooth, and add to it four tablespoonfuls of cream and a quarter of a pint of cold water with which one ounce of the best arrowroot has been mixed; stir till it boils, then colour with a little of Marshall's apple green, and add a quarter of a pint of maraschino syrup, two ounces of castor sugar, a dessertspoonful of Silver Rays (white) rum, and a saltspoonful of essence of vanilla, then rub through the tammy and use either hot or cold.

Silver Rays Rum Sauce.—Put into a stewpan six raw yolks of eggs, three raw whites of ditto, two ounces of castor sugar, one wineglass of Silver Rays (white) rum, and eight drops of Marshall's carmine, whip these briskly together for four to six minutes whilst the pan is standing in boiling water, when the sauce will present the appearance of a soufflé, and is ready for use. This is an excellent sauce to serve with plum-pudding, baba, soufflés, hot puddings, &c.

Vanilla Sauce.—To serve with puddings, iced soufflés, hot soufflés, and cake sweets for dinner, &c.—Put one and a half gills of new milk or cream into a stewpan with half a split vanilla pod, and two ounces of castor sugar to infuse in the bain marie for about fifteen minutes, then put six raw yolks of eggs into a basin and stir the infused milk on to them, then return the mixture to the fire until it becomes as thick

K
bon
toget
th cold
bove.

ADINESS.

(Some other Sauces are give… …pecial Dishes.)

Brown Sauce.—Fry four ounces of flour, four ounces o butter, four ounces of tomatoes, till a good brown colour, then add two quarts of good-flavoured stock made from cooked meat

Rubbing Sauces through the Tammy.

bones; stir till it boils, and let it boil till reduced one fourth part, keeping it well skimmed; then, when quite f fat, tammy. This sauce may always be ke being boiled up once or twice a w

Veloute Sauce.— one and a

Opposite Preparing fowl and game birds: from W. A. Henderson's *The Housekeeper's Instructor*, 1793.

This page Guides to the preparation of standard sauces: pages from *Mrs. A. B. Marshall's Cookery Book*, *c.* 1889. Mrs. Agnes Marshall ran a famous cookery school in Mortimer Street, central London.

LA TRUFFE
Chercheurs de truffes dans le Périgord.
Véritable Extrait de viande Liebig.
Reproduction interdite.
Voir l'explication au verso

GEWÜRZPFLANZEN.
Zimt. (Cinnamomum zeylanicum).
Blüte
LIEBIG COMPANY'S FLEISCH-EXTRACT.
Gesetzl. geschützt.
Siehe Rückseite.

Opposite Hunting truffles and harvesting spices: two more cards in the the Liebig series, *c.* 1912.

Above A cook and his larder: mezzotint by Richard Earlom, 1775, after a painting by Martin de Vos.

These pages Tinned foods and cuts of fresh meat, essential contents of the well-run larder.

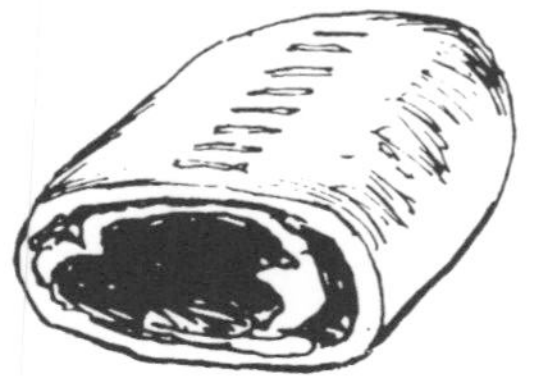

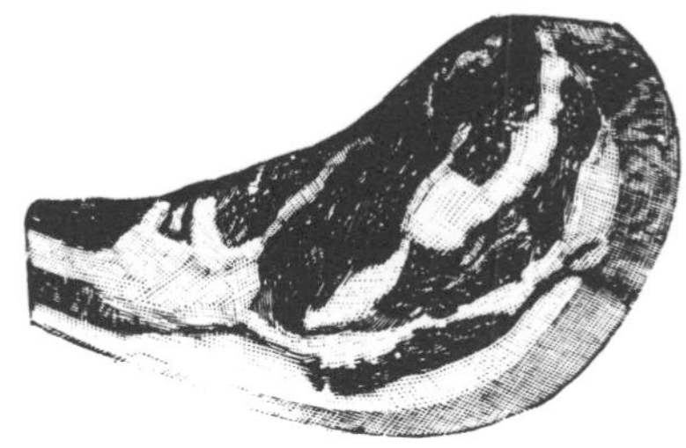

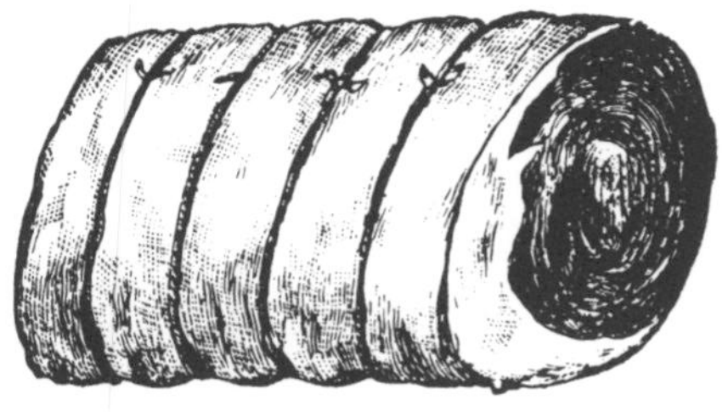

Overleaf The turn-of-the-century craze for meat extracts: measuring up to father, c. 1900, and a special Bovril advertisement from *The Graphic*, 1910.

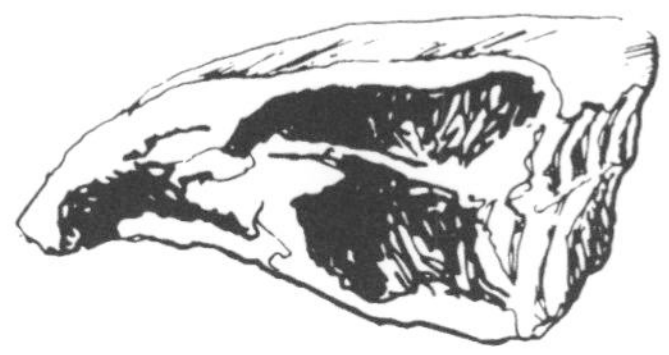

BOVRIL

-keeps you up to par

H H Harris

EASPOONFUL TO A
ING WATER & STIR
"BOVRIL"
BOVRIL LIMITED
LONDON
"Brother, where art thou?"

These pages More period gems from the store-cupboard.

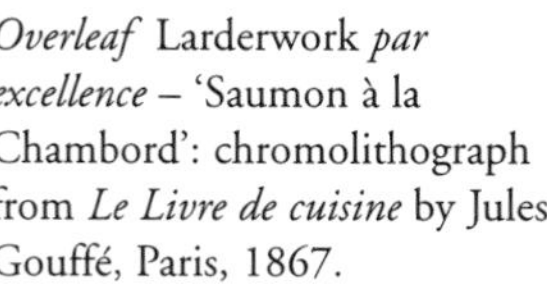

Overleaf Larderwork *par excellence* – 'Saumon à la Chambord': chromolithograph from *Le Livre de cuisine* by Jules Gouffé, Paris, 1867.

BEST
PICKLES

FAVORITE
BUCK-WHEAT

MASON'S
FRUITJAR

FAVORITE
SUCCOTASH

BEST
TOMATOES

PURE
VERMONT
Maple Syrup

SLICED
PINEAPPLE

YELLOW CRAWFORD PEACHES

CHOICE
GREEN GAGES

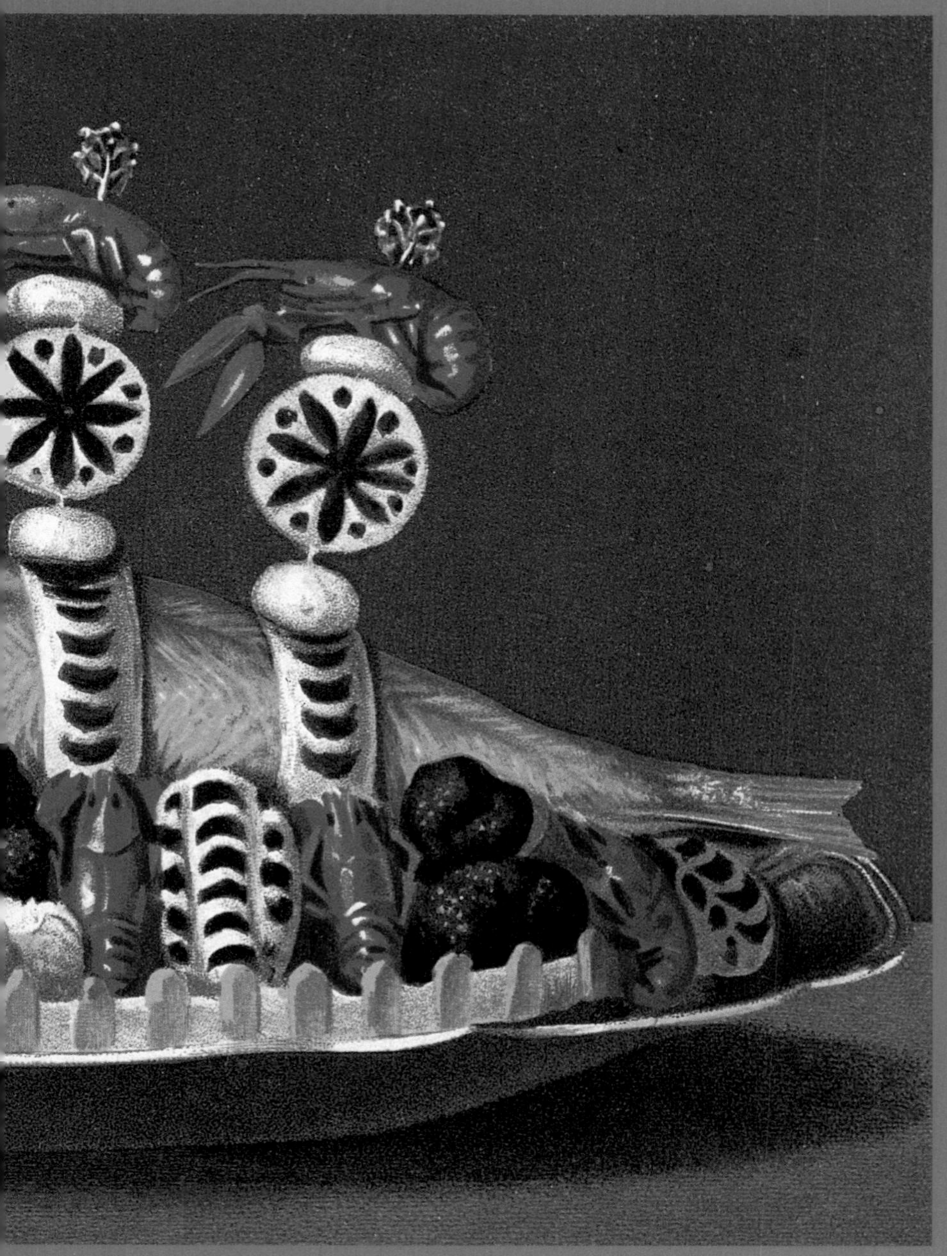

These pages Straight from the *potager*: a selection of leaf vegetables from nineteenth-century prints.

Above and *opposite* Varieties of edible mushrooms: chromolithographs by H. Furrer, Neuchâtel, *c.* 1870.

1.
2.
3.
4.
5.
6.
7.
8.
9.
10.
11.

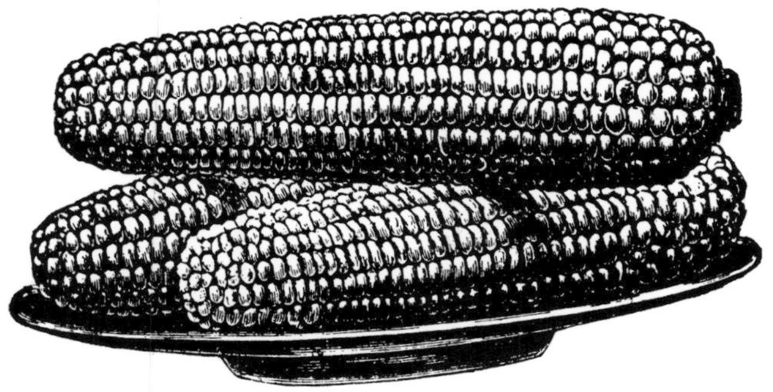

These pages The cornucopia of the kitchen garden: more arrangements from nineteenth-century prints.

These pages Assorted edible fungi, including mushrooms and truffles: chromolithograph, London, *c.* 1880.

These pages Set-pieces of the culinary art awaiting transfer to kitchen and table: nineteenth-century gastronomic elaboration.

Overleaf Various *hors-d'oeuvres*: chromolithograph from *Le Livre de cuisine* by Jules Gouffé, Paris, 1867.

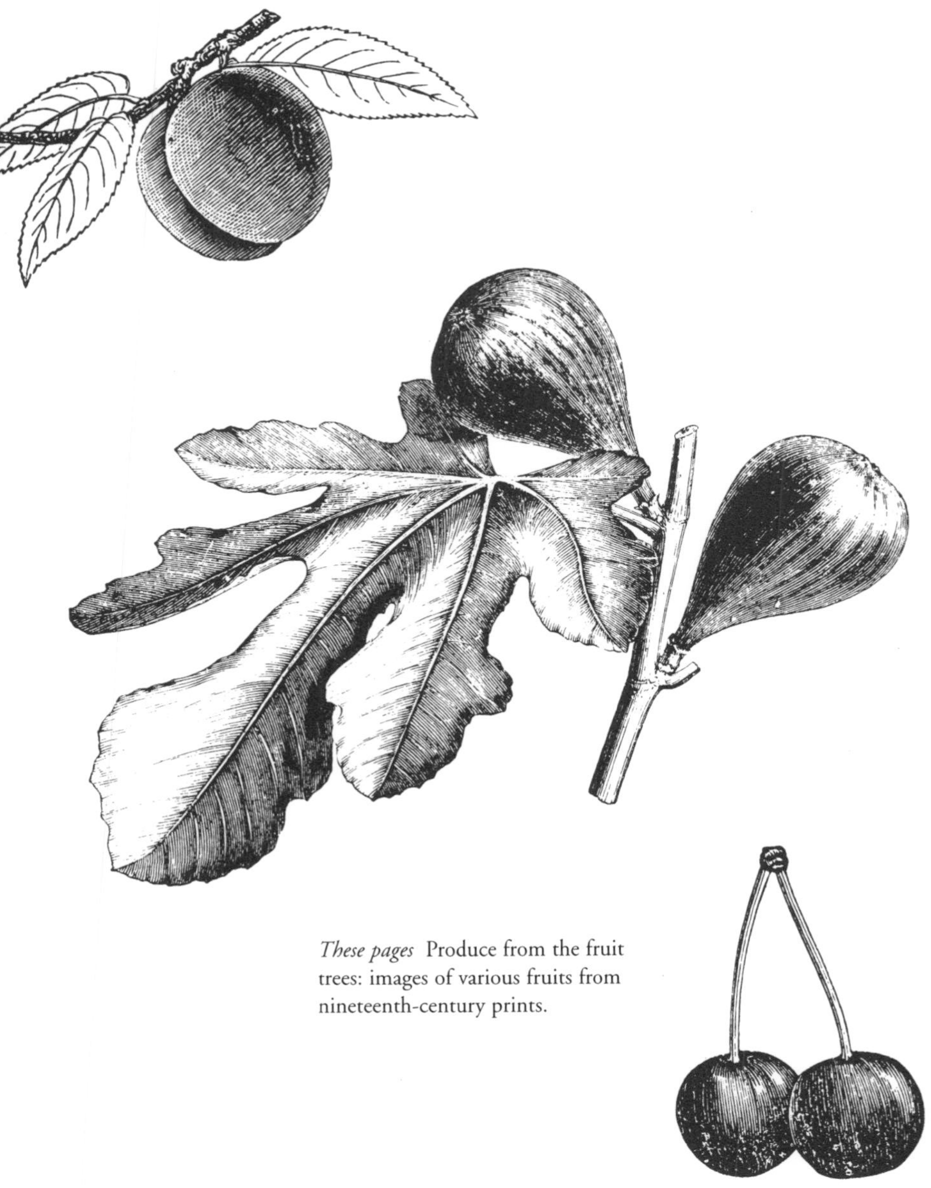

These pages Produce from the fruit trees: images of various fruits from nineteenth-century prints.

Above A selection of puddings from *Mrs. Beeton's Book of Household Management*, second and enlarged edition, 1869.

Opposite A selection of elaborate cakes: chromolithograph from *The Royal Book of Pastry and Confectionery*, 1874.

2
1
3
4
5
6
7
8

These pages Domestic fruits and some from further afield: the pineapple must have seemed quite exotic in the nineteenth century.

1
2
3
4
5
6
7
8
9
10

These pages A selection of pastries from *The Royal Book of Pastry and Confectionery*, 1874.

Above The art of the cake in the late nineteenth-century: to tempt any larder thief.

Opposite More fruits from Pierre-Joseph Redouté: *(clockwise)* apple, garden plum, hazelnuts and pomegranate.

This page More Liebig promotional cards, *c.* 1912; such jars of meat extract would certainly have figured among the contents of a turn-of-the-century larder or store cupboard.

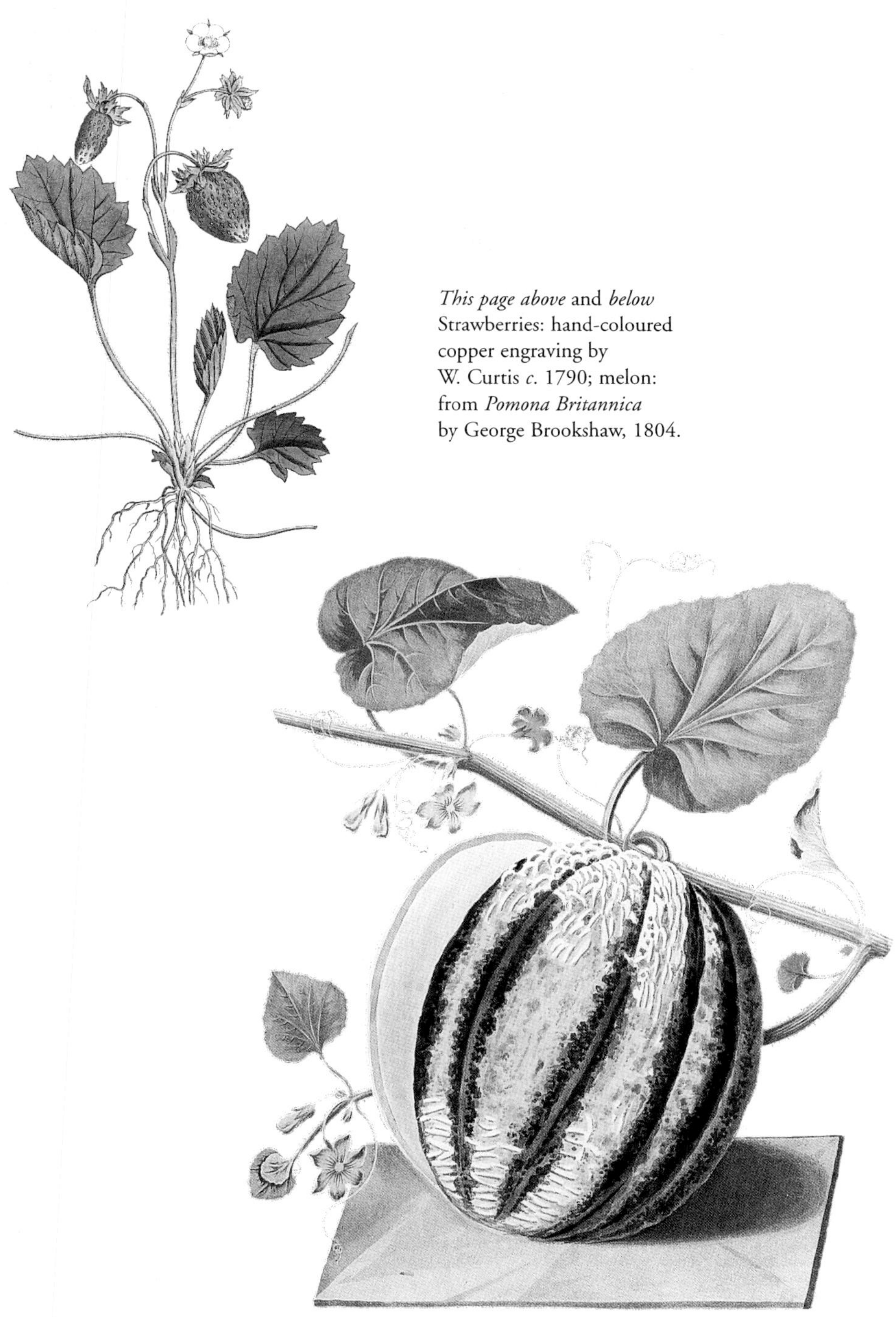

This page above and *below* Strawberries: hand-coloured copper engraving by W. Curtis *c.* 1790; melon: from *Pomona Britannica* by George Brookshaw, 1804.

Above Redcurrants: a plate by Pierre-Joseph Redouté, Paris, 1827–79.

Right Cherries: a plate from *Pomona Franconica*, Nuremberg, 1776–79.

Above 'Fresh fruit': chromolithograph plate issued with *The Illustrated London News*, 1860.

Overleaf 'The Golden Age': a copy of a picture exhibited at the British Institution in 1859, published with *The Illustrated London News*, 1861.

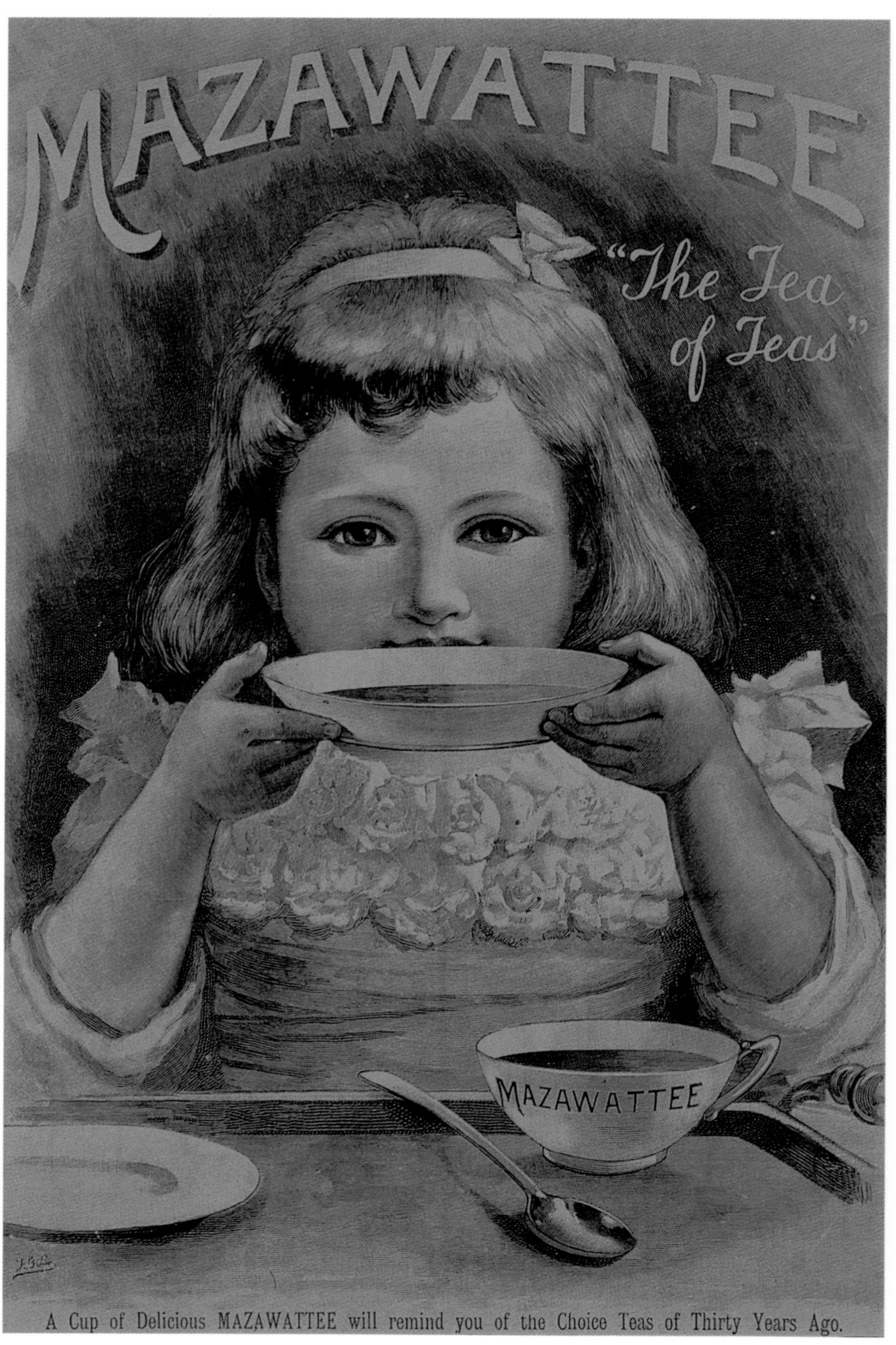
MAZAWATTEE
"The Tea of Teas"
MAZAWATTEE
A Cup of Delicious MAZAWATTEE will remind you of the Choice Teas of Thirty Years Ago.

Opposite 'The tea of teas': wood engraving advertisement from *The Illustrated Sporting and Dramatic News*, 1892.

Above 'Victorious over all others': advertisement from *The Graphic*, 1893.

"Sing out the praise of the cup that is cheering,
Not a head-ache or heart-ache is found in its brew."

Sounding the praises of

TETLEY'S TEAS.

Above and *opposite* 'The cup that is cheering...': advertisements for Tetley's Teas from a publicity booklet, Chicago, *c.* 1890.

AN AFTERNOON TEA
TETLEY'S TEA
INDIA & CEYLON
JOSEPH TETLEY & CO'S
SPECIAL BLEND TEA
TETLEY'S TEAS
LIKE GOOD CHILDREN
NEVER BEATEN.
Compliments of
SIEGEL, COOPER & CO.,
CHICAGO, ILL.
Where you can get a FULL LINE OF TETLEY'S TEAS.
COPYRIGHT.

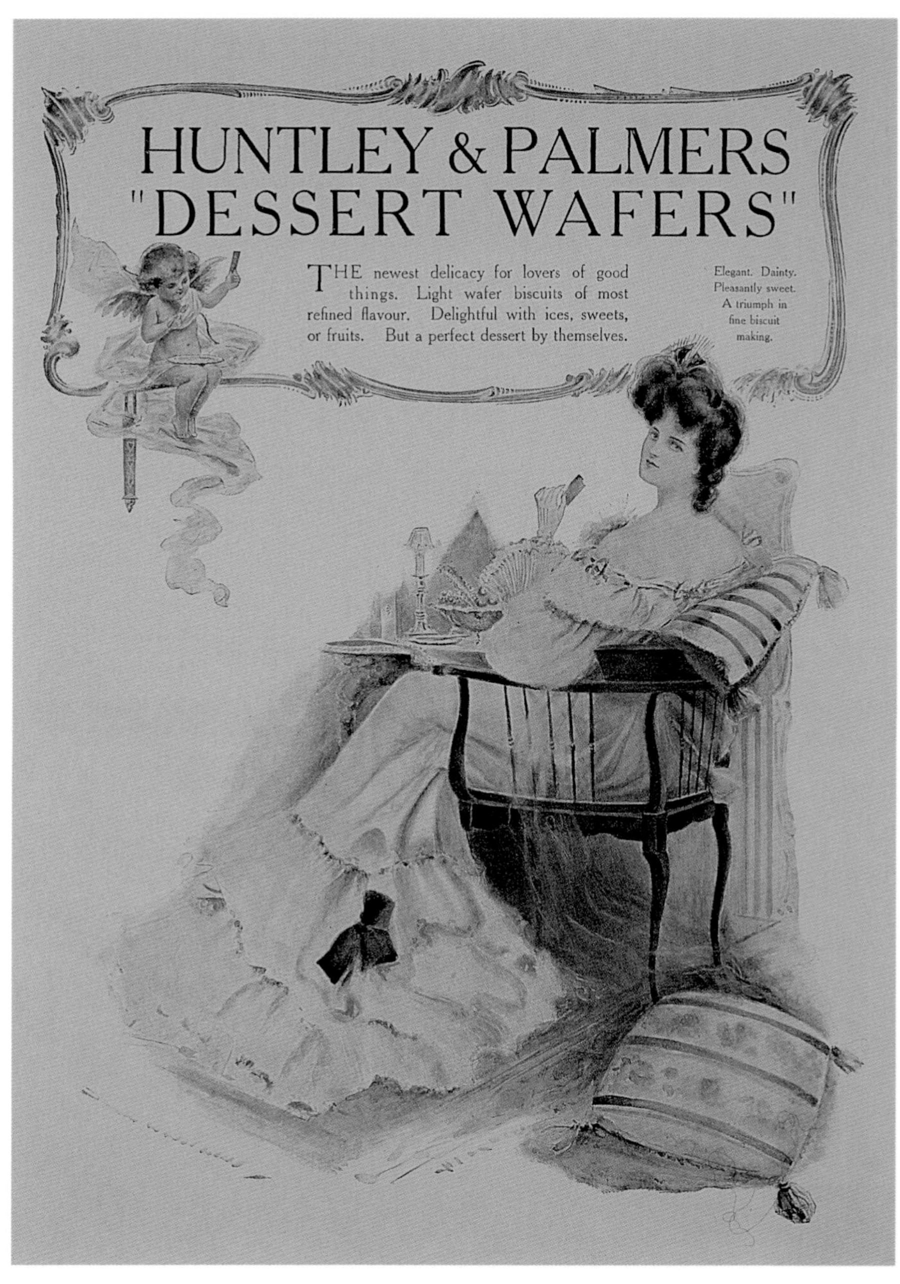

These pages Advertisements for dessert wafers and cocoa published in, respectively, *The Graphic*, 1905, and *The Illustrated Sporting and Dramatic News*, 1899.

These pages British and French advertisements, *c.* 1920, for, respectively, chocolates and pudding mixes.

DESSERTS DE LA FAVORITE
DESSERTS DE ROI
GATEAU DE RIZ
aux fruits confits
La Favorite
DROCOURT
QUATRE DÉJEUNERS
CACAO
PUR & SOLUBLE EN POUDRE
La Favorite
SUCRE VANILLÉ
La Favorite
FAVORITE VANILLE
MODE D'EMPLOI
La Favorite
FLAN
La Favorite
DROCOURT
LEVURE
La Favorite
DROCOURT
VANILLE BOURBON
La Favorite

BIRD'S CUSTARD Powder provides not only Delicious Custard, but an endless variety of delightful Dishes from the Recipes accompanying each Packet.

NO EGGS! NO RISK!!

N.B.—Ladies and housekeepers can add to their list of Dishes a number of choice Dainties for the Dinner and Supper Table by consulting a valuable little book, entitled "PASTRY AND SWEETS." It will be forwarded, GRATIS and POST FREE, on receipt of address, by ALFRED BIRD & SONS, DEVONSHIRE WORKS, BIRMINGHAM.

Opposite 'No eggs! No risk!': wood engraving advertisement for Bird's Custard Power, 1895.

This page More confections from the shelves of the nineteenth-century larder.

—4—

The Heat of the Kitchen

Mayhem and Mania in the Culinary Engine-Room

The kitchen of Brillat-Savarin was the apple of that distinguished gourmet's eye. After a splendid dinner given by him in 1825 to two guests and after allowing them to admire the original model for a bust and a portrait of his beautiful cousin, Madame Récamier, he treats them to a tour of the ingenious delights of his kitchen: his 'economical' stock-pot, his oven, his clockwork turn-spit and his steamer. The stock-pot, the *pot-au-feu*, expresses the very essence of the kitchen – that magical receptacle into which may be thrown left-overs, off-cuts and anything to hand to add to the basic stock, changing the contents to provide differing dishes from day to day.

The kitchen is the one room of the house or apartment where we expect to be looked after; its combination of heat and sustenance recall its long-ago ancestor, the communal cooking fire. It is associated with stir, bustle, warmth, richness and ripeness. It is the place which drives the rest of the establishment in which it is located, whether that be a

Opposite The kitchen help: wood engraving by W. J. Mosses after a drawing by Florence Gravier from *The Illustrated Sporting and Dramatic News*, Christmas Number, 1885.

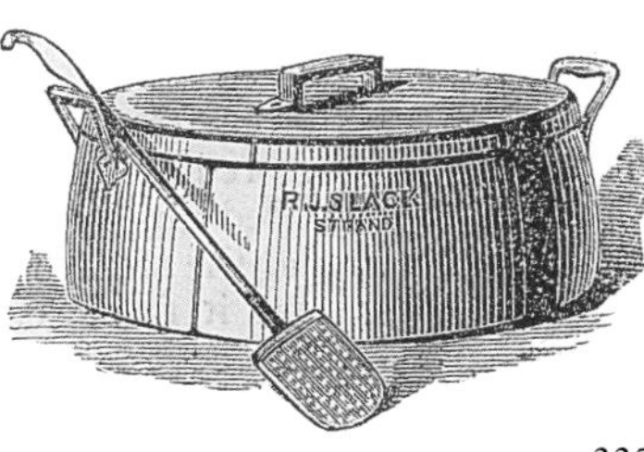

domestic environment, a club or restaurant, or a huge institution like Windsor Castle. All these varieties of kitchen are illustrated in the pages which follow. Yet it is the domestic variety which captures our affections. Indeed, the circumstances of modern urban living often re-emphasize the central role of the kitchen in our culture in that this is the place where many of us choose to eat, and where food may be served directly from the utensils of its preparation.

The kitchen table has a special importance, fulfilling a number of functions as a surface for food preparation and for eating. Who needs a dining-room if the kitchen and its table are large and well-organized? Of the two accoutrements of even the most basic life in Western cultures – the bed and the table – it might be said that the latter is the more important. It draws groups and families together and, in its

Left 'The Kitchen': eighteenth-century steel engraving by A. H. Payne after a painting by Caspar Netscheir (1639–84).

Opposite 'The Heat of the Kitchen': copper engraving from Florinus' *Œconomus Prudens*, Nuremberg, 1702.

kitchen incarnation, associates them not only with the consumption of food but also with its preparation.

The possibility, too, of antagonisms in the kitchen of the 'Too many cooks spoil the broth' variety made it an ideal vehicle for caricaturists. Their subjects, certainly during the nineteenth century, range from the amusing image of the monkey cook and his helpers (page 275) to political satire (pages 258-259), as the great powers of Europe seek to dominate the world situation, (i.e. the kitchen), underlining its role as the centre of all important matters. It may also be the place of passion, as the maid entertains her soldier friend (page 266) or (page 267) gives herself up to wine and song at a musical kitchen dresser!

'The Queen's Christmas' – the kitchen at Windsor Castle: engraving from *The Illustrated London News*, 1894.

Left The kitchen of 'a school of cookery' at the International Exhibition: wood engraving from *The Graphic*, 1873.

Overleaf The kitchen at Windsor Castle at Christmas: illustration by J. Brown for *The Illustrated Times*, 1857. 'Symmetrical rows of tables line the hall of Royal cookery; and here the white-jacketed and white-capped cooks (assisted sometimes by smart young damsels) are busily employed putting the finishing touches to the dainty dishes that are to be set before the Queen.'

This page The cooker of the future: wood engraving advertisement from *The Graphic*, 1897.

THE "ALBIONETTE" IS THE COOKER OF THE FUTURE!

THE only perfect Oil Cooking Stove, performs every Cooking operation *at one and the same time* at one-third the cost of COAL or GAS. Heat regulated to a nicety.

Lit and Extinguished in a moment. **"Our Latest and Best,"**

The result of 25 *years' experience.*

All other Oil Stoves are now old-fashioned.

Sold by all Stores and Ironmongers. Prices from 27s. to 90s. Illustrated Catalogue free, from

Rippingille's Albion Lamp Co., BIRMINGHAM.

ORIGINAL Inventors of Oil Cookers. Contractors to H.M. Government.

London Depot and Show-rooms: 65, HOLBORN VIADUCT, E.C.

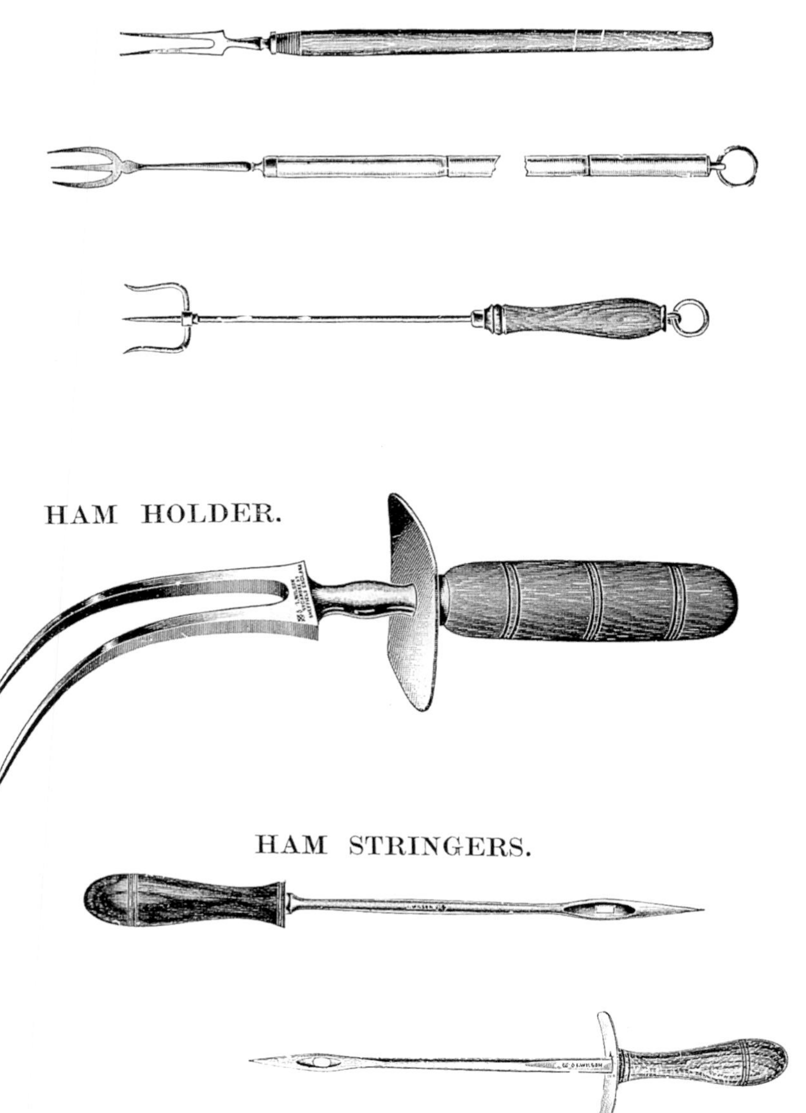

This page Utensils for holding and stringing ham: from the catalogue of John Wilson (Sheffield) Ltd., *c.* 1930.

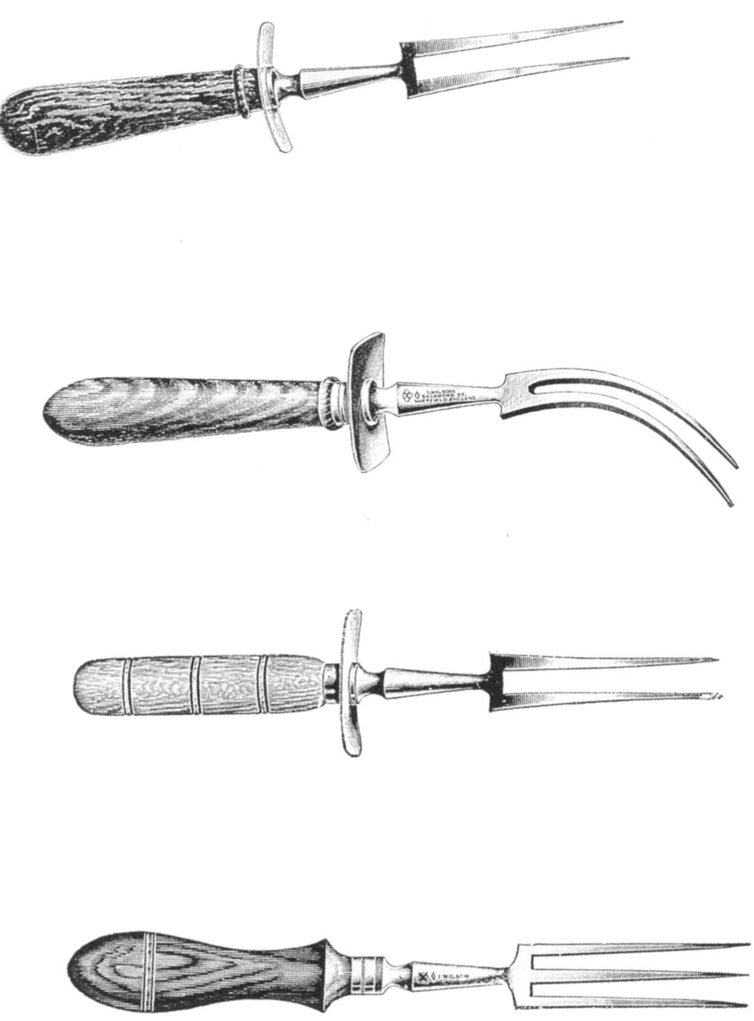

Above and *opposite* Stainless steel forks for ham and beef, cleavers and choppers: from the catalogue of John Wilson (Sheffield) Ltd., *c.* 1930.

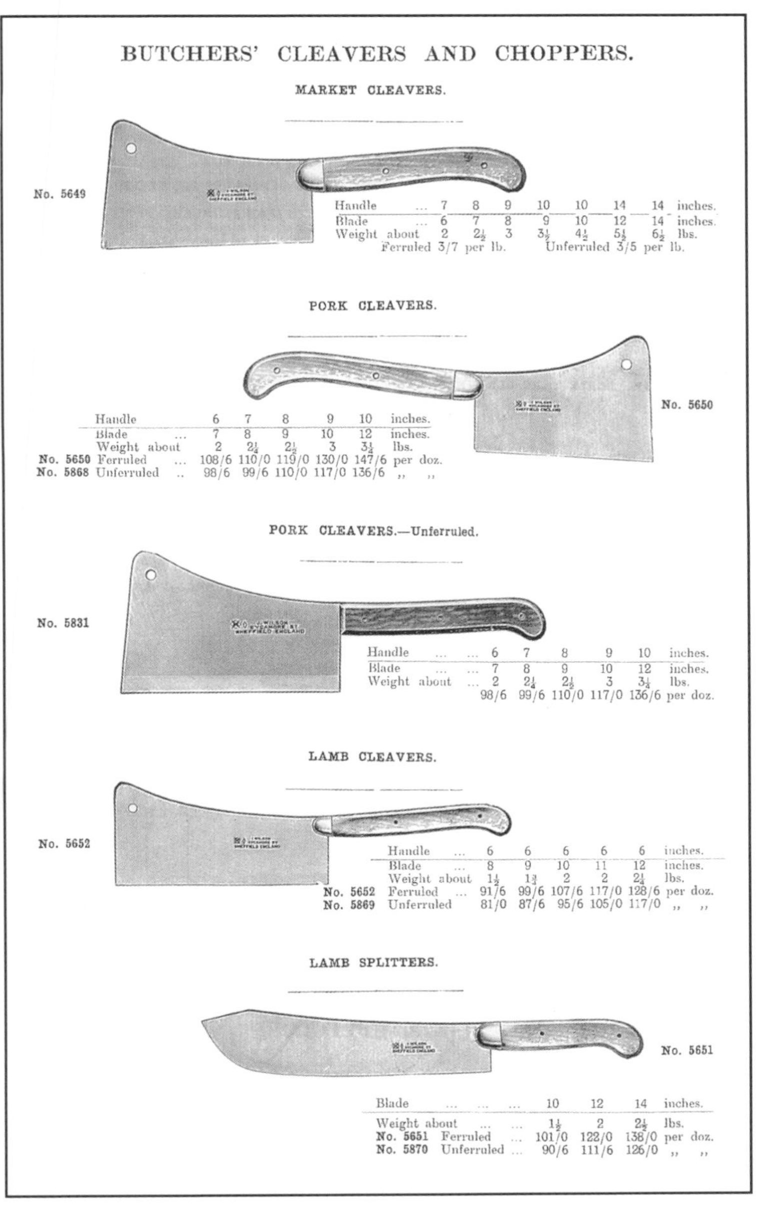

BUTCHERS' CLEAVERS AND CHOPPERS.

MARKET CLEAVERS.

No. 5649

Handle ...	7	8	9	10	10	14	14	inches.
Blade ...	6	7	8	9	10	12	14	inches.
Weight about	2	$2\frac{1}{2}$	3	$3\frac{1}{2}$	$4\frac{1}{2}$	$5\frac{1}{2}$	$6\frac{1}{2}$	lbs.

Ferruled 3/7 per lb. Unferruled 3/5 per lb.

PORK CLEAVERS.

No. 5650

	Handle	6	7	8	9	10	inches.
	Blade ...	7	8	9	10	12	inches.
	Weight about	2	$2\frac{1}{4}$	$2\frac{1}{2}$	3	$3\frac{1}{4}$	lbs.
No. 5650	Ferruled ...	108/6	110/0	119/0	130/0	147/6	per doz.
No. 5868	Unferruled ..	98/6	99/6	110/0	117/0	136/6	,, ,,

PORK CLEAVERS.—Unferruled.

No. 5831

Handle	6	7	8	9	10	inches.
Blade	7	8	9	10	12	inches.
Weight about ...	2	$2\frac{1}{4}$	$2\frac{1}{2}$	3	$3\frac{1}{4}$	lbs.
	98/6	99/6	110/0	117/0	136/6	per doz.

LAMB CLEAVERS.

No. 5652

	Handle ...	6	6	6	6	6	inches.
	Blade ...	8	9	10	11	12	inches.
	Weight about	$1\frac{1}{2}$	$1\frac{3}{4}$	2	2	$2\frac{1}{4}$	lbs.
No. 5652	Ferruled ...	91/6	99/6	107/6	117/0	128/6	per doz.
No. 5869	Unferruled	81/0	87/6	95/6	105/0	117/0	,, ,,

LAMB SPLITTERS.

No. 5651

	Blade	10	12	14	inches.
	Weight about	$1\frac{1}{2}$	2	$2\frac{1}{2}$	lbs.
No. 5651	Ferruled ...	101/0	122/0	138/0	per doz.
No. 5870	Unferruled ...	90/6	111/6	126/0	,, ,,

The 'ideal kitchen' of the late nineteenth century: anonymous engraving.

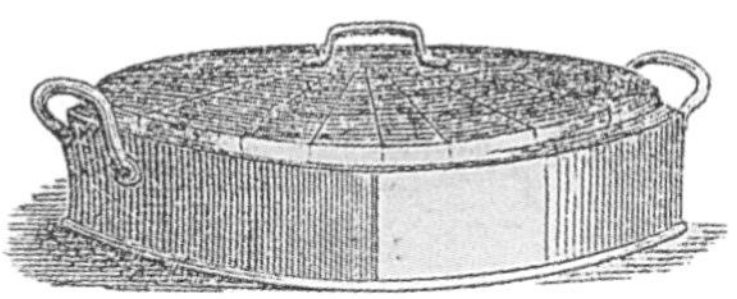

Above Kitchen utensils: illustrations from *Mrs. Beeton's Book of Household Management*, second and enlarged edition, 1869.

Right The kitchen of the Reform Club, London: engraving by Edward Radclyffe, *c.* 1850.

492 THE ILLUSTRATED LONDON NEWS Nov. 9, 1867

THE PARIS INTERNATIONAL EXHIBITION.

APPARATUS AND PROCESSES OF VENTILATING, WARMING, COOKING, AND LIGHTING (CLASS 24).

COTTAGER'S COOKING-STOVE, BY C. BOUCHER AND CO., AT FAMAY, ARDENNES.

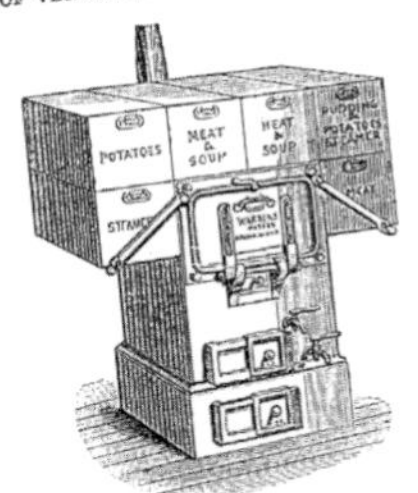

CAPTAIN WARREN'S PATENT COOKING APPARATUS THE ARMY AND NAVY.

COOKING APPARATUS OF GODIN-LEMAIRE, GUISE, AISNE.

The metal toys exhibited by M. Debors, just outside the court, are very good. Knives, forks, dinner services, and every description of dolls' plate, both in metal and china, are to be seen here. Several of the specimens are in aluminium bronze; and these, from the beauty and goldlike appearance of the metal, are most attractive. A few of the moulds used in the manufacture of these articles are also exhibited. The little toilet services have great charms for children; they are so nicely made; and, though superior to most, are not quite so elaborate as some in the neighbouring cases. At the top of this stall, though so high as to be almost invisible from the reflection of the glass, is a set of remarkably good fur animals. It is a pity that they are so much out of sight.

The miscellaneous toys of M. Simon are certainly superior to his dolls already mentioned. The horses and jockeys are nicely made, also the military toys, including the soldiers' tent. A remarkable canteen is placed here, though its size and general arrangement make it more fit for practical use than for the imaginary requirements of dolls.

The playthings exhibited by M. Schutz are different from all others in the Exhibition. They have some sort of movement, though not a clockwork one. This is managed either by the wheels setting parts in motion or by strings passing through the figures. A cart full of animals at the bottom of this case makes a capital toy. The animals can be taken in and out, and as the cart is pulled along a monkey goes through various comic evolutions. Every variety of figure is to be seen—dancing-men, monkeys, grotesque dolls, &c.; all are well finished and tastefully dressed. About the best toys here are two peasants made to represent hawkers, carrying large baskets of household wares on their backs. These baskets can be packed and unpacked, and so form an amusing toy.

M. Rémond has a few miscellaneous toys, besides dolls, which, however, form the more important part of his case. A mechanical train is conspicuous, as also some fair carts, horses, and military toys. In the centre of the court is a round table, on which the prolific top exhibited by M. Caumière is continually spun by an attendant. This top is of Japanese origin; and the number and variety of ways in which it may be spun, and the skill required in spinning it, make it quite an attractive plaything, even to grown-up people. Amongst the French miscellaneous toys, though placed in class 91, owing to their cheapness, must be included the exhibits of the following makers:—M. Feliker, a collection of the cheapest and fairly made toys, such as rough dolls, rattles, whips, &c.; M. Clavel, a number of wooden toys, such as cannons with large wheels, windmills, trumpets, &c., all quoted by the gross, at wonderfully low prices; M. Thael, animals made in plaster, of very original and grotesque shapes; M. Bunant, gutta-percha articles, including dolls, balls, rattles, &c.; and, lastly, a number of children's colour-boxes, of all prices and sizes, warranted to contain no poison. Little thumb-palettes, with half a dozen colours and a brush attached, sold for about 1½d., are likely to be popular.

Games.—There are only one or two unimportant French games exhibited among the toys; and these are by M. Giroux, who has an elaborate display, in class 26, consisting of a small cabinet with

REVOLVING STOVE-GRATE, BY GODIN LEMAIRE, OF GUISE.

RICHARDS' CIRCULAR-FRONT COOKING-STOVE IMPROVED AND MANUFACTURED BY W. BARTON, OF BOSTON, LINCOLNSHIRE.

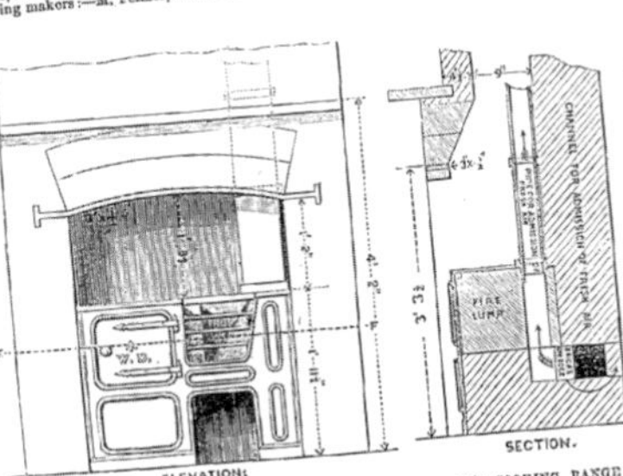

LARGE COOKING-RANGE BY M. VAILLANT, OF METZ.

PLAN AT E.F.

CAPTAIN DOUGLAS GALTON'S COOKING RANGE FOR MARRIED SOLDIERS.

AKERLAND'S COTTAGER'S WARMING AND COOKING STOVE (SWEDISH).

Opposite Cooking stoves exhibited at the Paris International Exhibition: wood engraving from *The Illustrated London News*, 1867.

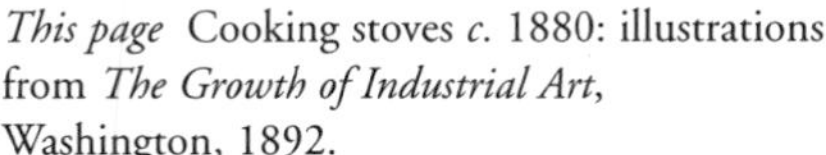

This page Cooking stoves *c.* 1880: illustrations from *The Growth of Industrial Art*, Washington, 1892.

'The Innocent Maid': lithograph by H. Jesson after a painting by C. Forster, London, *c.* 1850.

A ferocious-looking cook at work in his magnificently equipped kitchen: woodcut, Germany, *c.* 1540.

Chaos at the kitchen table – the fox steals the chicken: illustration from Goethe's *Reinecke Fuchs* by Wilhelm von Kaulbach, steel engraving, *c.* 1850.

Below Under the greenwood tree – a very primitive kitchen: woodcut, *c.* 1580.

Above Another kitchen disaster: copper engraving of a decorative capital from Florinus' *Œconomus Prudens*, Nuremberg, 1702.

Cooking pots and *bain-maries*: illustrations from Jules Gouffé's *Le Livre de cuisine*, Paris, 1867.

Overleaf A Victorian charterhouse kitchen: wood engraving, 1867.

Allemande-
Espagnole
Béchamel-
Maigre
Suprême

Above The kitchen: copper engraving, frontispiece to *The Housekeeper's Instructor* by W. A. Henderson, 1793.

Opposite Frontispiece to *The Complete Housewife* by Eliza Smith, copper engraving, 1773.

CUCINA INGLESE
LIRE STERLINE
MONIZIONI
MARINA
MARE EGEO
ROMENI
GRECO
RAGOUT
MARINATA ALLA BOSFORO
PANE TRIESTINO

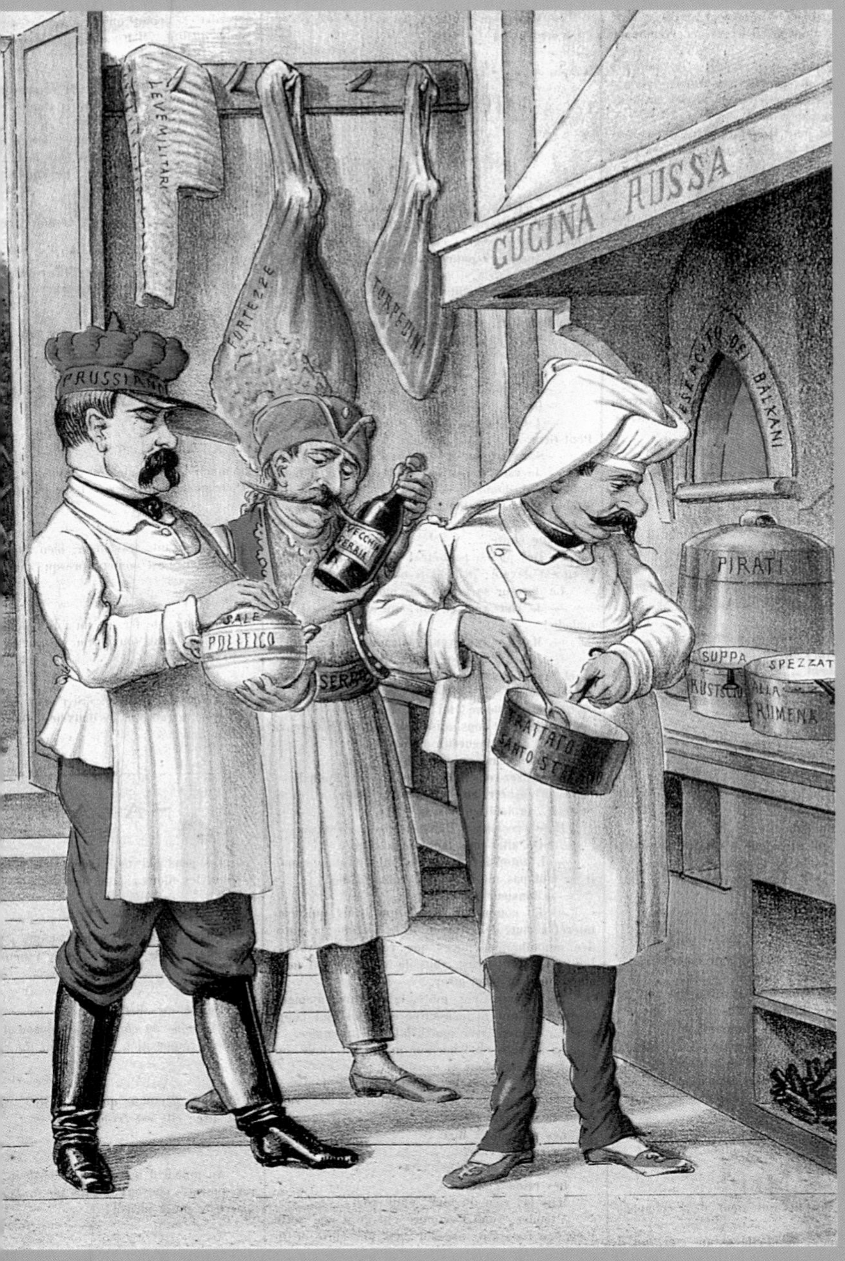
CUCINA RUSSA
LEVE MILITARI
FORTEZZE
TORPEDINI
ESERCITO DEI BALKANI
PIRATI
SALE
POLITICO
SUPPA
ALLA
RUMENA

Preceding pages Too many cooks spoil the broth – a comment on the aggressive intentions of the European states: coloured lithograph issued with the Italian review *Papagallo*, May 1878.

Right The specialist kitchen – at the heart of a bakery: steel engraving from a German book of trades, *c.* 1850.

Overleaf The British and Russians dispute the great bowl of polenta (Asia), while other nations wait for their morsel: coloured lithograph issued with the Italian review *Papagallo*, July 1877.

TIROLO
ISTRIA
MALTA
NOTE

COSTANTINOPOLI
D.POL
VITTORIA
SIA
POLITICA
SER
BO

Left 'Interior of a well-ordered kitchen': copper engraving frontispiece to *Le Cuisinier Parisien*, third edition, by B. Albert, Paris, 1825.

Opposite Spoons and skimmers for the kitchen: illustration from *Le Livre de cuisine* by Jules Gouffé, Paris, 1867.

N° 305. (Nouvelle série.) 20, rue Bergère, 20. Prix : 10 cent.

PETIT JOURNAL POUR RIRE.

Directeur-Gérant, A. Bourgain. AUX BUREAUX DU Mon Vve Philipon et Cie.

JOURNAL AMUSANT, du PAPIER COMIQUE, du MUSÉE COSMOPOLITE, etc.

FANTAISIES PARISIENNES, — par A. Grévin.

N° 974. 1021 P. J.

— Il me semble vous avoir déjà signifié, Fanchette, que je ne voulais plus voir de militaires dans votre cuisine!

— Plifotrékmatamifiin.

Opposite 'No soldiers in the kitchen!': illustration for the *Petit Journal Pour Rire* by A. Grévin, *c.* 1880.

Above Advertisement for Tregear & Co., makers of musical dressers, *c.* 1870.

1
2
3
3
4
5
11
12
12
12
13
WALMSLEY

Soyer's miniature kitchen, fitted up on board a steam-vessel by Messrs. Bramah Prestige of Piccadilly, under the guidance of Mr. Soyer of the Reform Club: wood engraving from *The Illustrated London News,* 1847.

This page Liebig cards, *c.* 1912, showing national kitchens: French, German and Chinese.

Above Strüdel-time in a German kitchen: chromolithograph by Albert Kretschmer, 1870.

Left The kitchen maids' tipple: lithograph, France, *c.* 1850.

Opposite Mischief in the kitchen: print published by Lemercier, Paris, *c.* 1850.

Opposite and *above* Animal crackers: a fox raid while cook's back is turned: steel engraving by Wilhelm von Kaulbach for Goethe's *Reinecke Fuchs*, *c.* 1850; monkey business: lithograph after a painting by Alexandre-Gabriel Decamps, *c.* 1830.

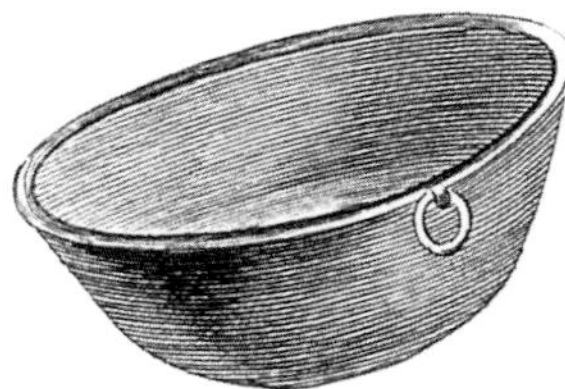

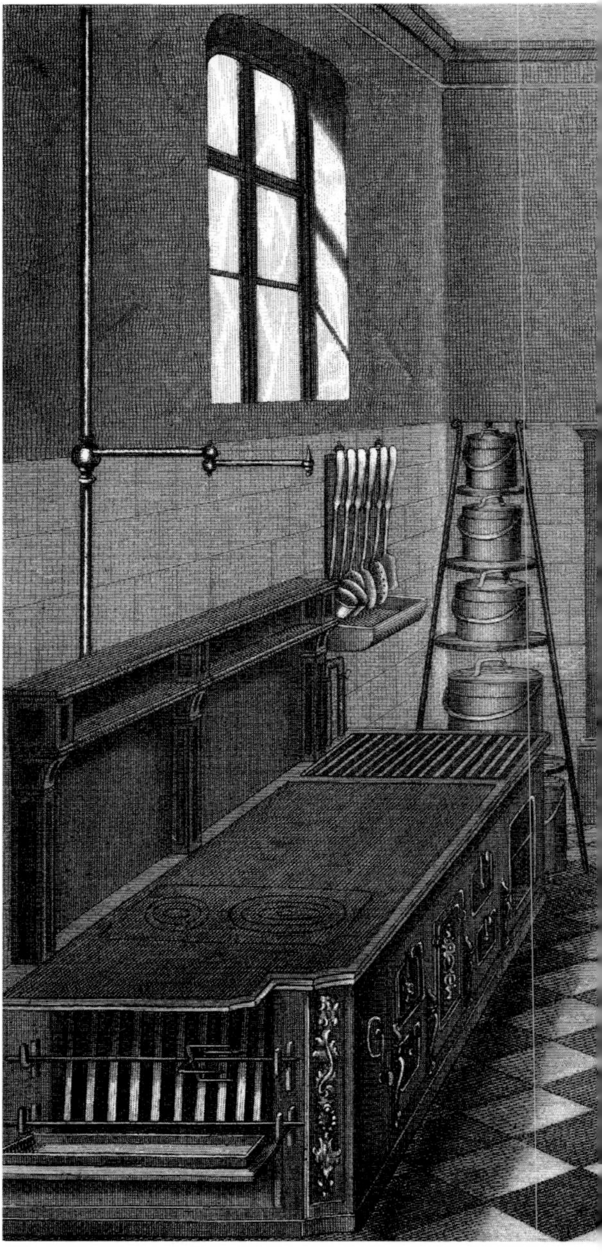

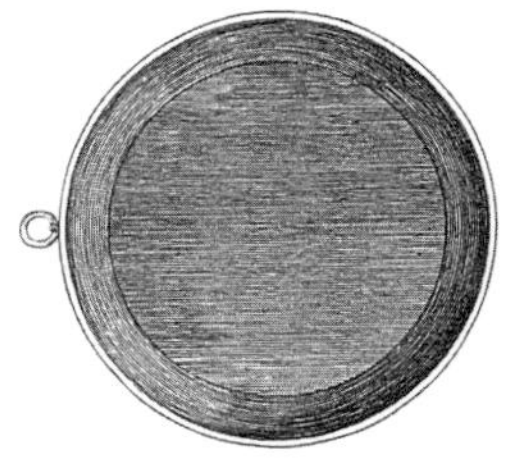

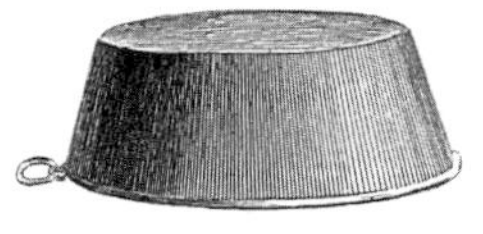

Above An 'ideal kitchen' for a late nineteenth-century refectory: anonymous print.

FRESH
BARM.

Opposite and *above* Courting the kitchen maids at the inn: lithographs, Germany, *c.* 1850.

The Flemish cook – apparently overwhelmed by every variety of fish, game and meat: copper engraving after a painting by David Teniers, *c.* 1750.

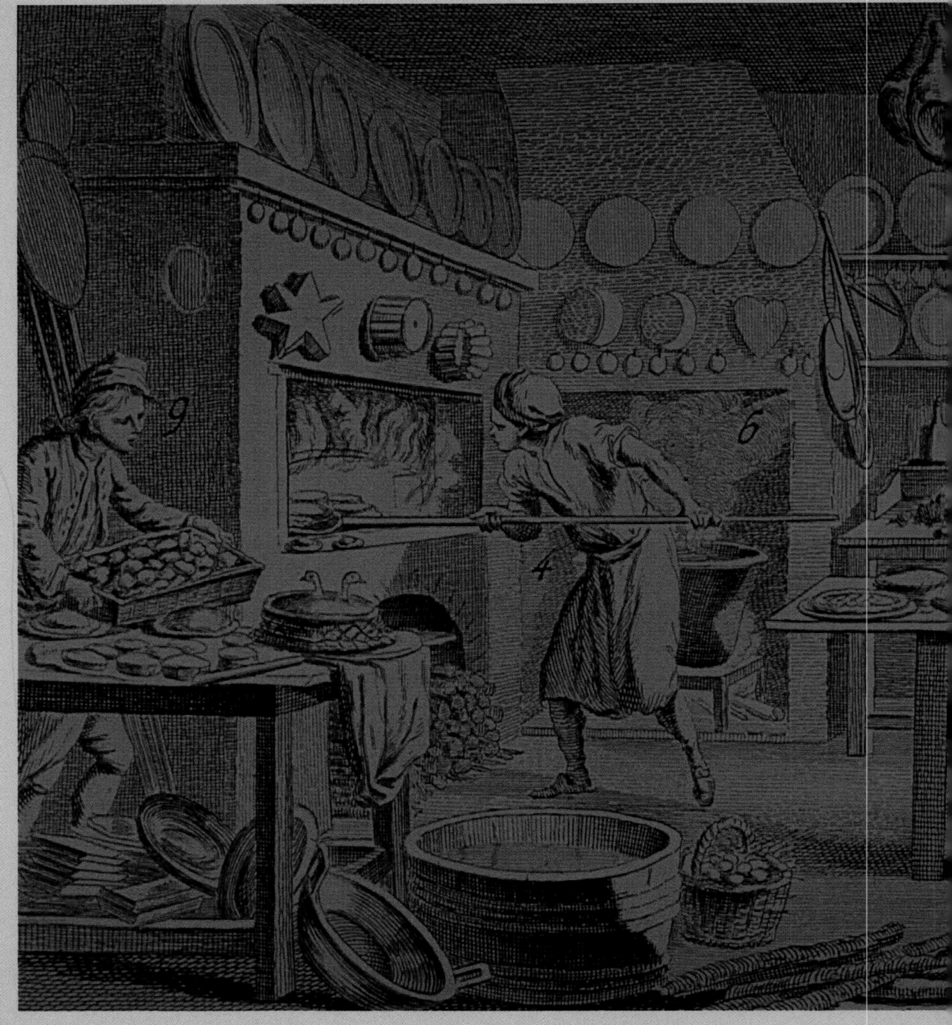

5
7
8
3
2

Preceding pages and *above* Kitchen scenes: copper engravings from Florinus' *Œconomus Prudens*, Nuremberg, 1702.

Preceding pages Hell's Kitchen: Richie & McCall's preserved meats plant, Houndsditch, London: wood engraving from *The Illustrated London News*, 1852.

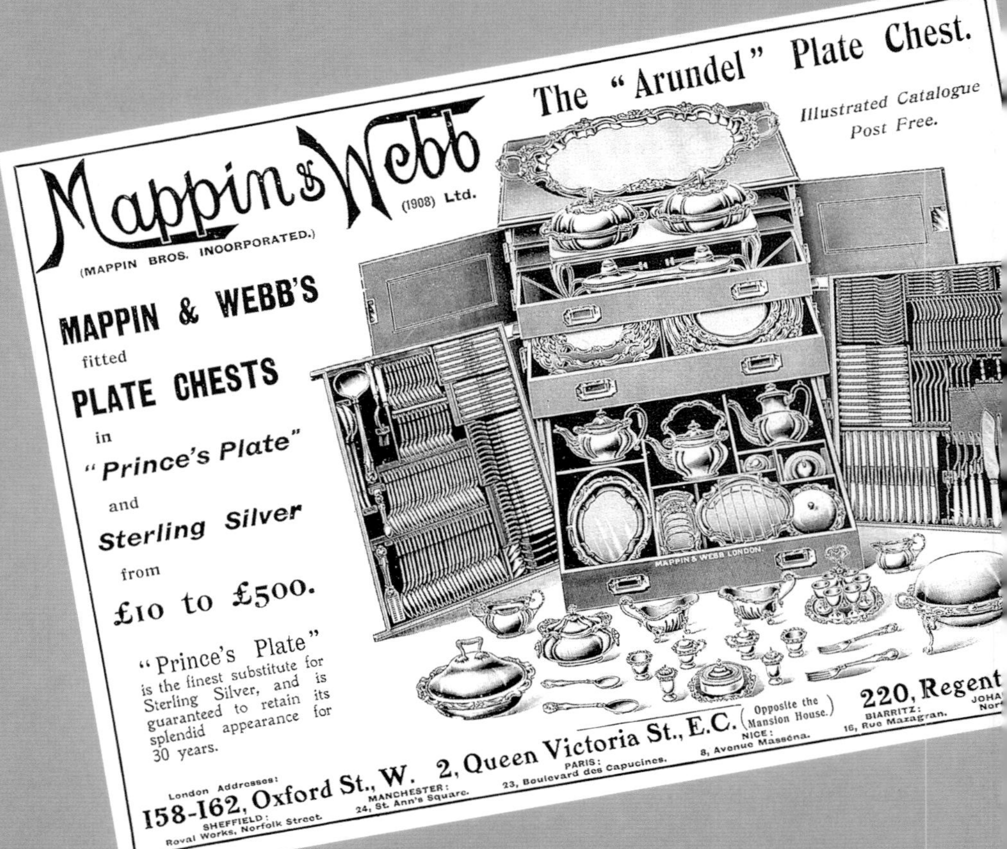

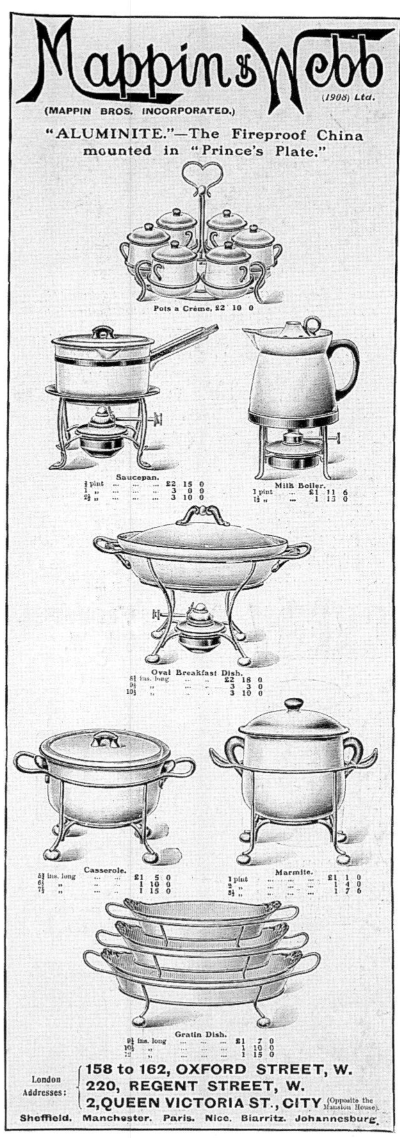

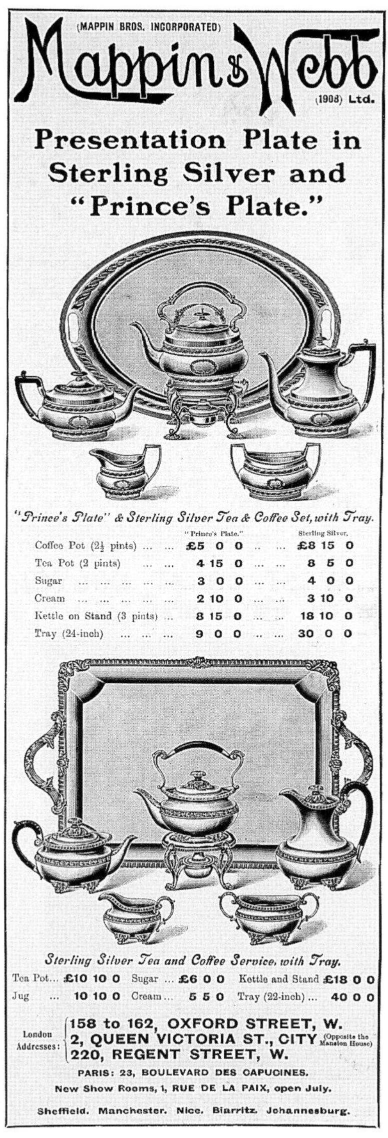

Mappin & Webb's kitchen and table wares: advertisements from *The Illustrated London News* and *The Illustrated Sporting and Dramatic News*, 1909.

28 *Advertisements.*

MOULDS FOR HOT & COLD ENTREES & SAVOURIES.

No. 215B.
BUTTERFLY MOULD.

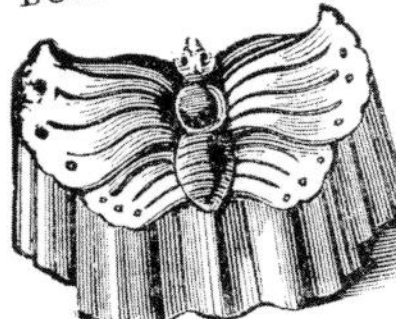

4*s*. 6*d*. per doz.

No. 215C.
FANCY MOULD.

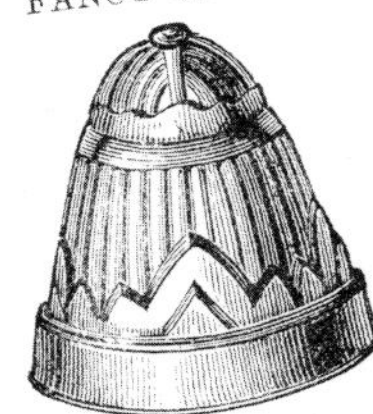

Copper tinned,
8*s*. per doz.

No. 215D.
FANCY MOULD.

Copper tinned,
8*s*. per doz.

No. 215E.
FANCY MOULD.

Copper tinned,
8*s*. per doz.

No. 215F.
FANCY MOULD.

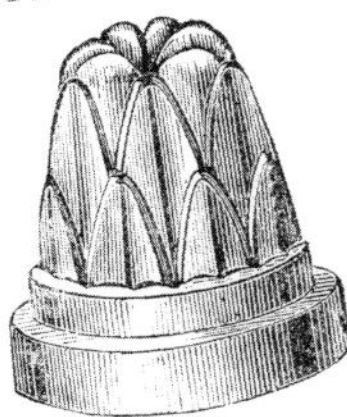

Copper tinned,
8*s*. per doz.

No. 215G.
FANCY MOULD.

Copper tinned,
8*s*. per doz.

No. 215H.—COPPER BOMBE.

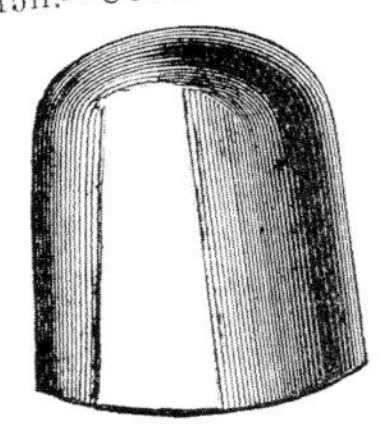

9*s*. per doz.

No. 217.—FLUTED FLEUR RING.

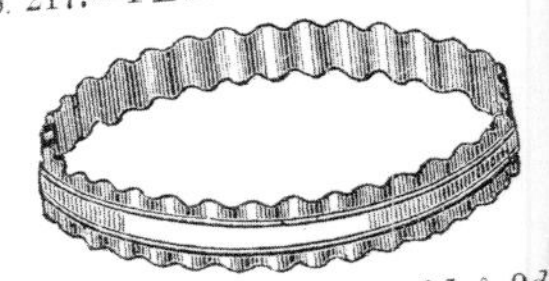

1*s*. each. Plain Fleur Rings, 6*d*. & 9*d*

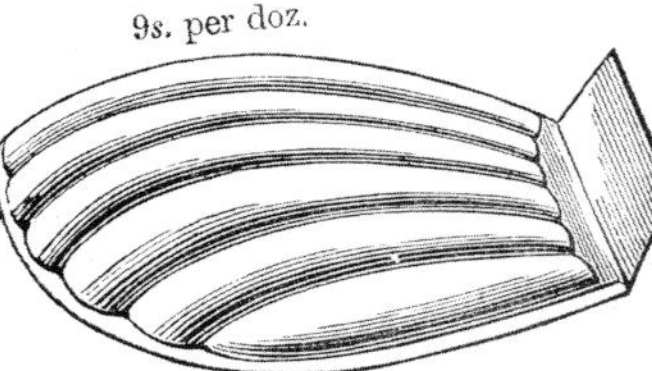

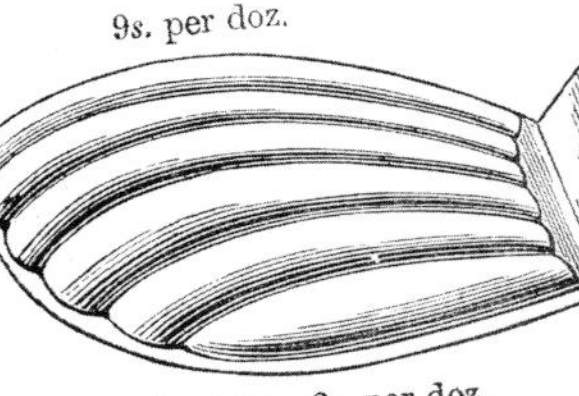

No. 209.—2*s*. per doz.

No. 215I.
WALNUT MOULDS

For Petits Fours, etc., 1*s*. 6

SPECIMEN PAGE FROM 'BOOK OF MOULDS.'

Advertisements. 25

MRS. A. B. MARSHALL'S SCHOOL OF COOKERY.

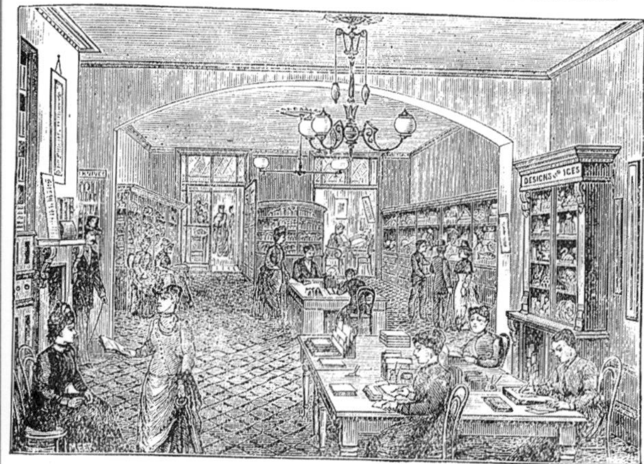

SHOW ROOM for Moulds, Cooks' Knives, Cutlery, &c.

THE BOOK OF MOULDS

May be had gratis on application, or is sent post free to any address.

IT CONTAINS

68 PAGES AND OVER 400 ENGRAVINGS.

STRATING, IN DIFFERENT SIZES AND DESIGNS, ABOUT

ISAND KINDS OF MOULDS.

OLLOWING SPECIMEN PAGES.

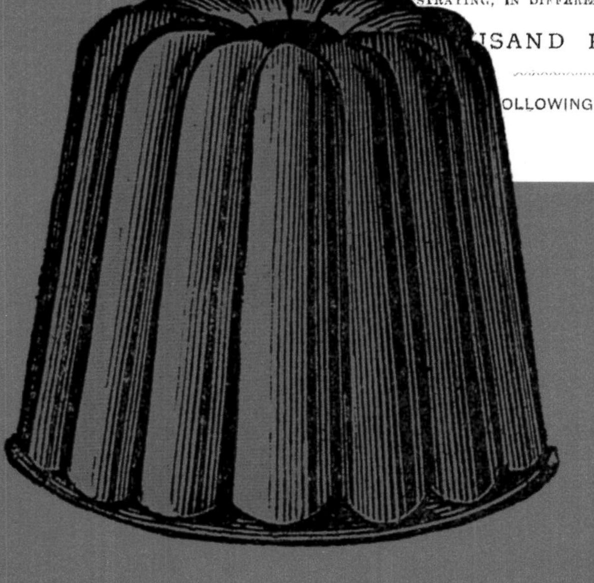

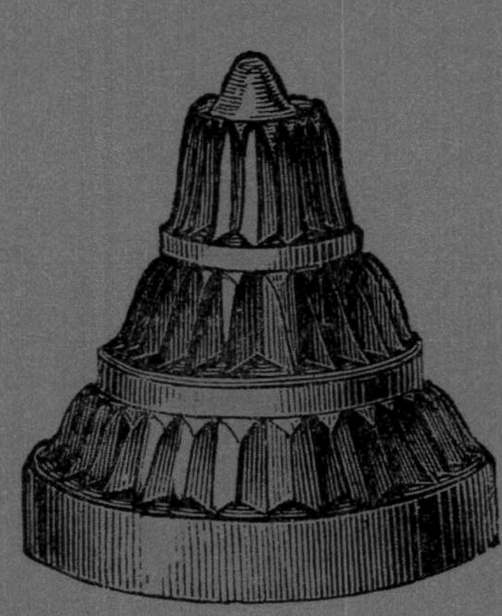

MRS. A. B. MARSHALL'S SCHOOL OF COOKERY.

IORTIMER STREET, W.

AND FRENCH, ITALIAN, AND
D WINES AND SPIRITS.
ACE, WELLS STREET, W.

at the cheapest price compatible
es and Price Lists free.

GIVEN FREE
ISHINGS OF KITCHENS
the requirements of

COOKERY

; often supplied by those who have no practical
The prices of any of the articles sold in this
of any of the large 'Stores.'

RANGES.

manufacturers' prices. No charge is made
d to meet the requirements of any household.
ome for another, a great amount of annoy-
dvice before selecting, as, naturally enough,
persuade the purchaser that his is the best.

KERS.

made as for Kitchen Ranges. Mrs. A. B.
all the leading kinds, and, moreover, has
ooks who have been her pupils.

MOULDS FOR HOT & COLD ENTRÉES & SAVOURIES.

No. 202.—FISH MOULD.

$4\frac{1}{2}$ in., 4*s*. 6*d*. per doz.

No. 203.—CRAWFISH.

$3\frac{1}{2}$ in., 4*s*. 6*d*. per doz.

No. 204.—CHICKEN.

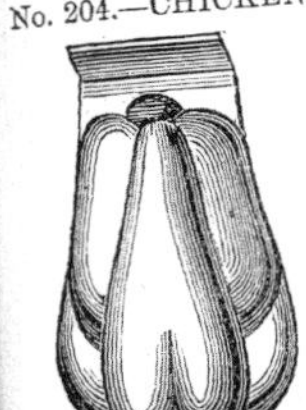

$2\frac{1}{4}$ in., 4*s*. 6*d*. per doz.

No. 205A.—TONGUE.

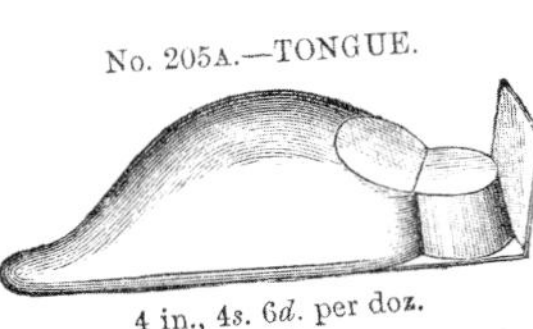

4 in., 4*s*. 6*d*. per doz.

No. 206.—HAM.

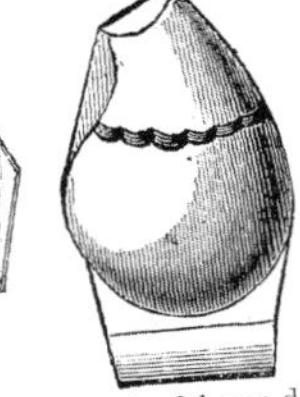

2 in., 4*s*. 6*d*. per doz.

No. 207.
FANCY BOUCHE CUPS.

4*s*. 6*d*. per doz.

No. 205.—COPPER EGG.

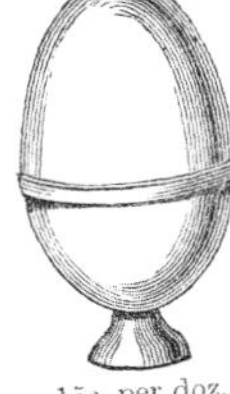

15*s*. per doz.

No. 208.
COPPER BOUCHE CUPS.

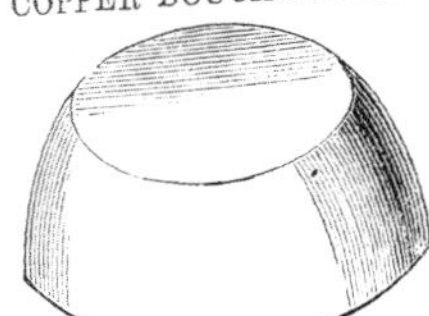

2 in. diam., 8*s*. doz.; tin, 2*s*. doz.
Tin, without indent, 1*s*. 4*d*. doz.

No. 215.—SMALL BOAT CUP.

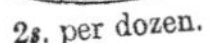

2*s*. per dozen.

No. 208A.

Copper tinned, 15*s*. per doz.

SPECIMEN PAGE FROM 'BOOK OF MOULDS.'

Preceding pages and *these pages* Moulds for various purposes – 'every kitchen requisite supplied at the cheapest price compatible with quality!': from the catalogue of Mrs. A. Marshall's establishment in Mortimer St., London, *c.* 1890.

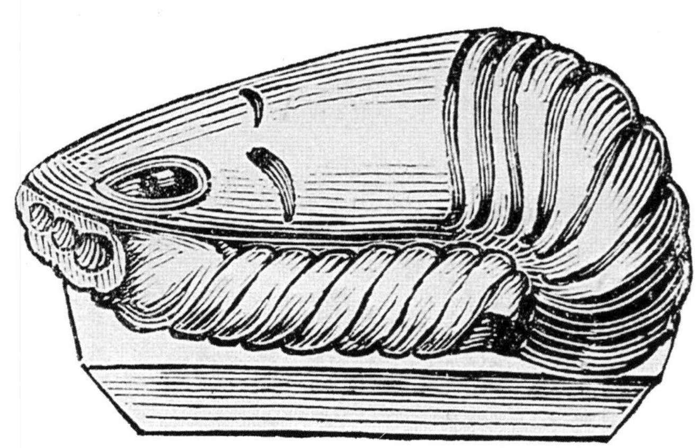

HÔTEL
CONTINENTAL
RUE
DE
Castiglione
RUE DE RIVOLI
PARIS

5

Table Matters and Manners

The Arts of Gastronomy

Of all the stages in the journey of our food from cultivation and rearing to its appearance at the point of consumption, it is the latter which is most set about with rituals and customs, with secrecy and hidden agendas. And it is the supposedly orderly universe of the table which provides us with the majority of the images in this chapter.

There are many threats to this universe, as some of the grotesque excesses illustrated on the following pages remind us. The attendant ghosts of bad behaviour or intimations of impending disaster have lurked close to many a famous banquet (The Last Supper being perhaps the best known example). Indeed, the evolution of the way meals are served and of their accoutrements – crockery, cutlery, and so on – can be seen in terms of an attempt to exclude disruption from the table. Pointed knives were eventually replaced by ones with rounded ends; during the nineteenth century meals came to be seen as a succession of courses, the so-called 'Russian style' (page 337), limiting con-

Opposite Advertising the dinner menu of the Hôtel Continental, Paris, *c.* 1870.

tact with other people at the table, something well-nigh impossible during the eras when dishes were placed all over the table and diners helped themselves as best they could. Again, the table is a focus for good and orderly behaviour, with its attendant complex system of 'manners' and protocol. There are now other threats to this orderly scene which would have bewildered Brillat-Savarin: lack of time to plan and prepare well-constructed meals, and the diminution of the importance of the table as the centre of group and family life by the intrusive advent of the 'TV dinner'.

A number of the pages which follow show eighteenth-century subjects, seemingly synonymous with gastronomic excess, although in no way rivalling the legendary banquets given by the notoriously self-indulgent Roman senator, Lucullus. Brillat-Savarin himself had a particular affection for the age of Louis XV; we suspect, however, that even the healthiest of modern-day appetites would balk at this menu of 1740 for ten people: first course – *bouilli*, an entrée of

veal cooked in its own juice, an *hors d'œuvre*; second course – a turkey, a platter of vegetables, a salad, a *crême* (occasionally); dessert – cheese, fruit, preserves.

Some of the most wittily elegant imagery of this chapter is that of the restaurant menu cards, especially those from France. They are colourful, amusing, occasionally salacious. The scenes of restaurant life, too, provide often amusing interludes: the table of lawyers (page 362); the misery of eating alone (page 319 and pages 360-361); the *table d'hôte* (pages 300-301 and pages 372-373), precursor of the restaurant (the place where one went to get better – hence the name).

But enjoyment is the dominant theme of this book; the celebration of plenty. Manic, if you will. And a suitable end-note in that spirit might be to quote the menu of the Frères Provençaux restaurant, splendidly illustrated on page 378, as observed by Brillat-Savarin: 12 soups, 24 *hors d'œuvres*, 15 or 20 beef entrées, 20 mutton entrées, 30 entrées of chicken or game, 16 or 20 of veal, 12 pâtisseries, 24 fish dishes, 15 roasts, 50 side dishes, 50 desserts. And so, ranging from the disgustingly gross (pages 372–373) to the magnificently formal (pages 326–327), these images of consumption end the chain which began in fields and plantations, on quaysides and in markets, and now terminates *à table*.

These pages The interior of a Venetian café: print after a painting by S. Melton Fisher, exhibited at the Royal Academy, London, published as a special supplement to *The Graphic*, 1889; fish knives: from the catalogue of Joseph Elliot & Sons, Sheffield, *c.* 1930.

Five o'clock tea in Paris: colour print from a painting by Pierre-Georges Jeanniot, published as a special supplement to *The Graphic*, 1900.

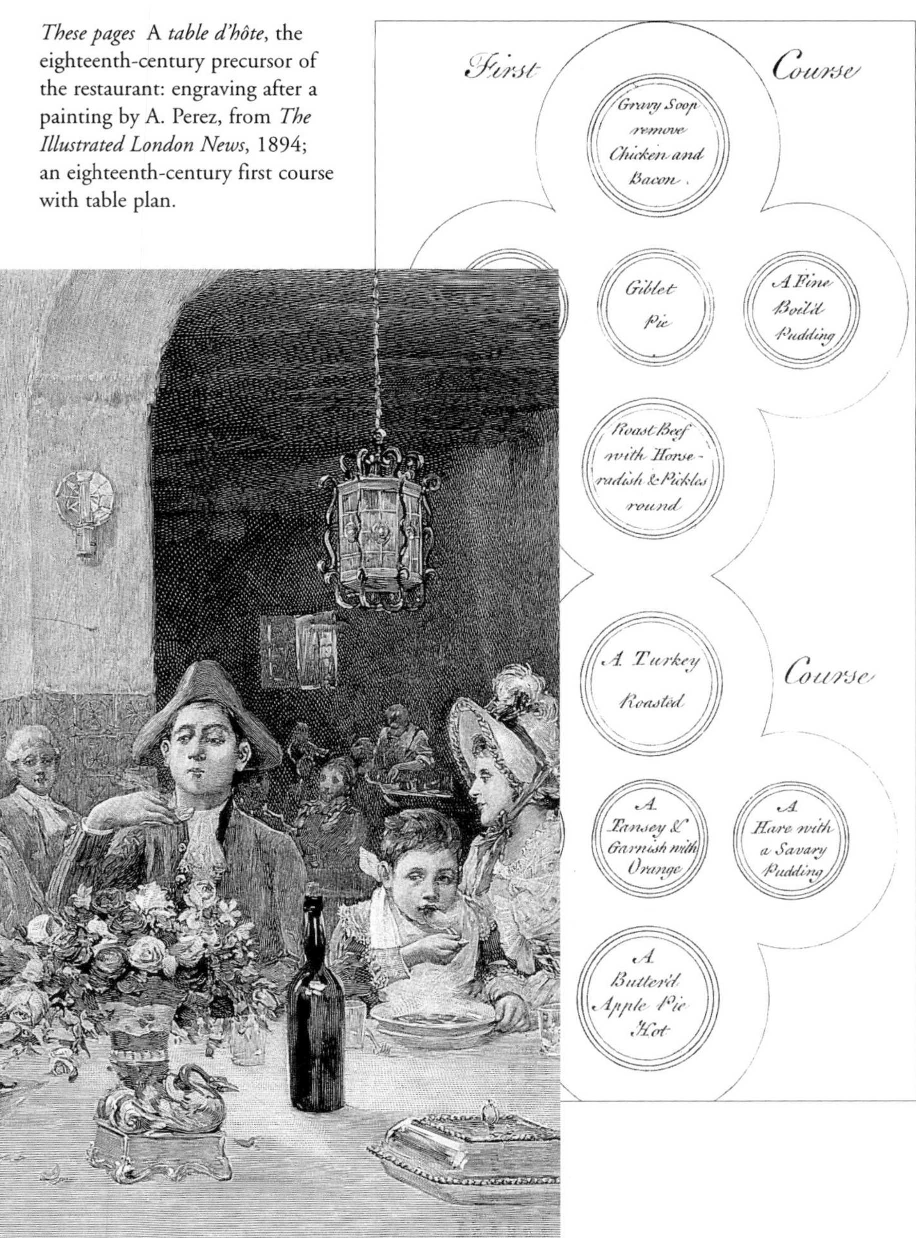

These pages A *table d'hôte*, the eighteenth-century precursor of the restaurant: engraving after a painting by A. Perez, from *The Illustrated London News*, 1894; an eighteenth-century first course with table plan.

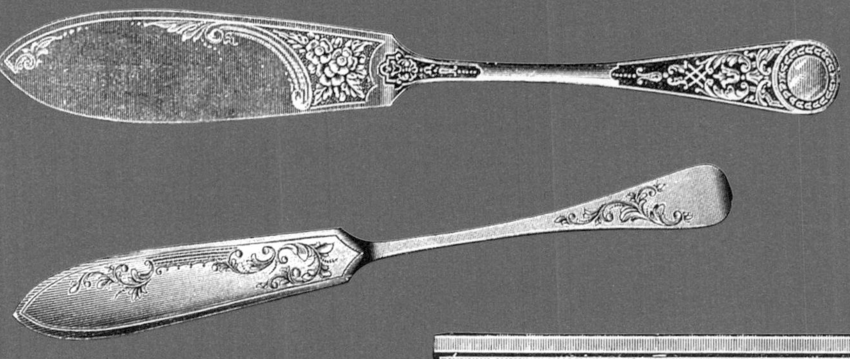

These pages Cutlery, mainly for fish: from the catalogue of Joseph Elliot & Sons of Sheffield, c. 1930.

CORPORATE
J ✠ C
MARK.

Joseph Elliot & Sons, Sheffield,

Manufacturers of CUTLERY, SILVER, and ELECTRO-PLATE.

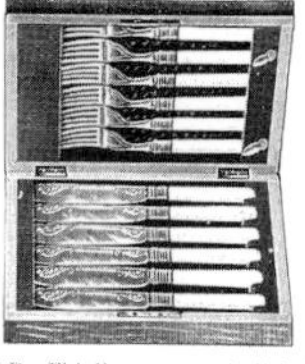

P1053.
Leather Case, containing 6 pairs Dessert Knives and Forks.

	per case.
Xylonite Handles,	35/-
Ivory Handles,	47/-
Pearl Handles,	48/-

N.B.—Fish Eaters to match, Xylonite Handles, 37/- per case.
Ivory Handles, 47/-

P789. Engraved Handles, as above, Five o'clock size,
6 Tea Spoons, 1 pair Sugar Tongs, in case.. 20/-
12 Tea Spoons, 1 pair Sugar Tongs, in case.. 33/-

P799. Fancy Stamped Handles, Five o'clock size,
6 Tea Spoons, 1 pair Sugar Tongs, in case.. 15/6
12 Tea Spoons, 1 pair Sugar Tongs, in case.. 29/-

ALL PRICED 12 PAIRS IN WALNUT TOP LOCK-UP CASE.

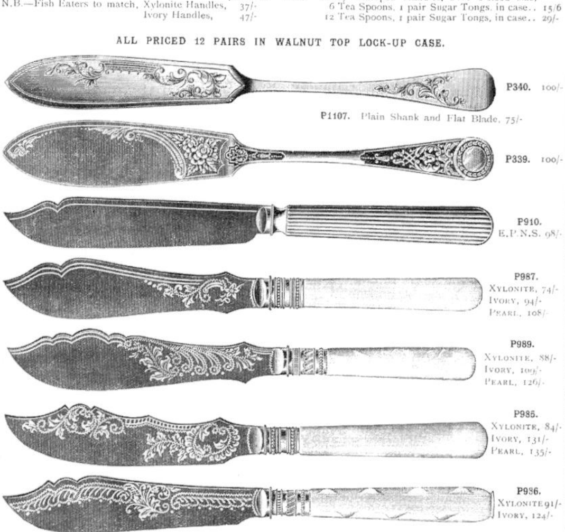

P340. 100/-

P1107. Plain Shank and Flat Blade, 75/-

P339. 100/-

P910.
E.P.N.S. 98/-

P987.
Xylonite, 74/-
Ivory, 94/-
Pearl, 108/-

P989.
Xylonite, 88/-
Ivory, 109/-
Pearl, 126/-

P985.
Xylonite, 84/-
Ivory, 131/-
Pearl, 135/-

P986.
Xylonite 91/-
Ivory, 124/-

N.B.—Six pairs in case can be supplied at proportionate prices.

16

Joseph Elliot & Sons, Sheffield,

Manufacturers of CUTLERY, SILVER, and ELECTRO-PLATE.

ALL CARVERS HAND FORGED AND DOUBLE SHEAR STEEL.

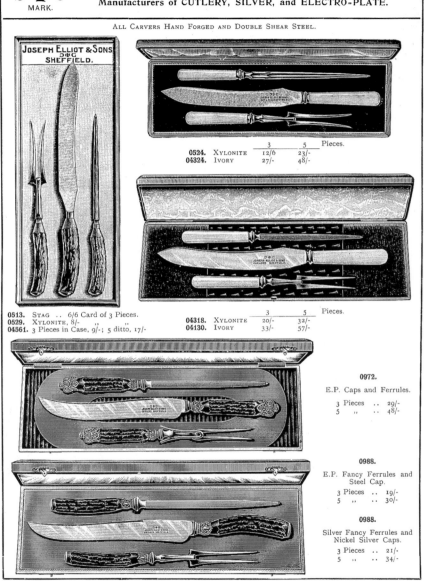

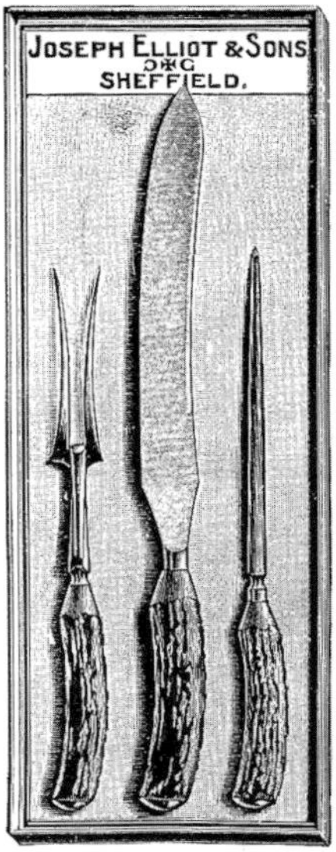

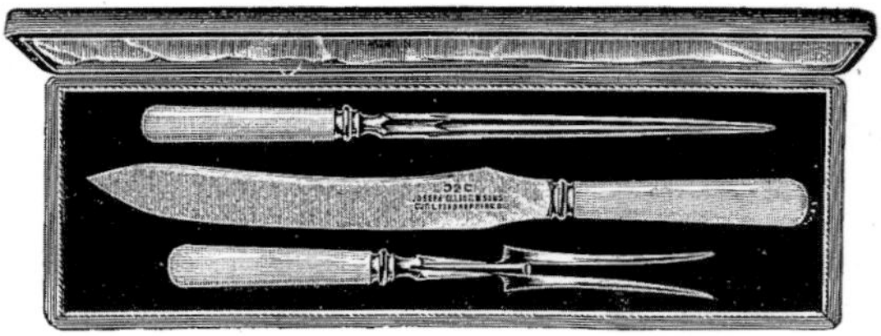

		3	5 Pieces.
0524.	XYLONITE	12/6	23/-
04324.	IVORY	27/-	48/-

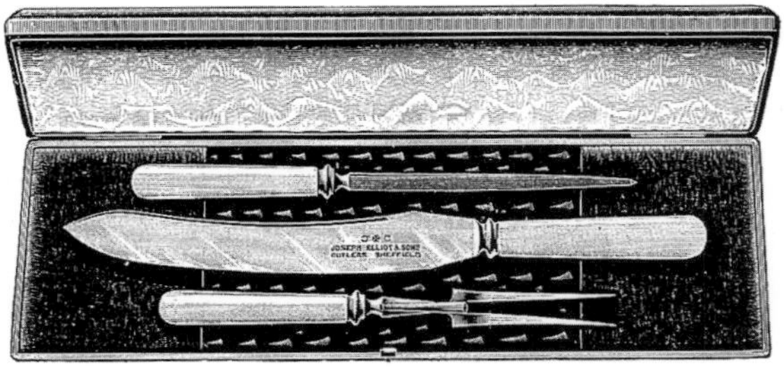

0513. STAG .. 6/6 Card of 3 Pieces.
0529. XYLONITE, 8/- ,, ,,
04561. 3 Pieces in Case, 9/-; 5 ditto, 17/-

		3	5 Pieces.
04318.	XYLONITE	20/-	32/-
04130.	IVORY	33/-	57/-

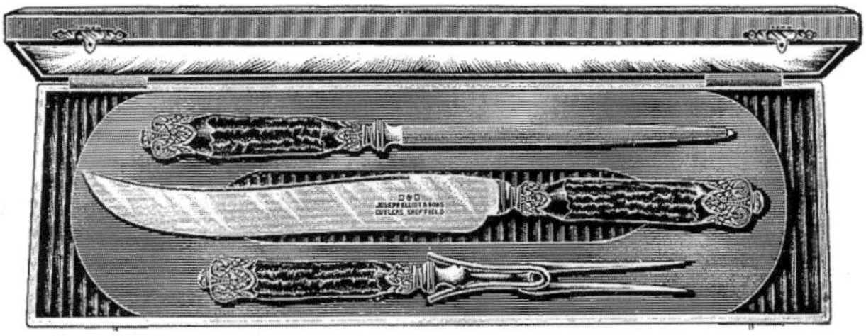

0972.

E.P. Caps and Ferrules.

3 Pieces .. 29/-
5 ,, .. 48/-

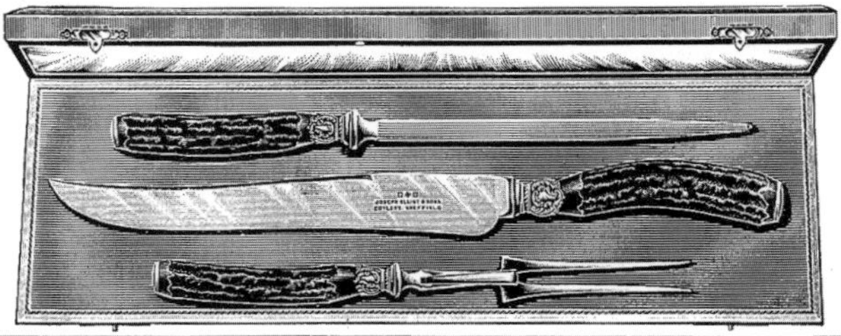

0988.

E.P. Fancy Ferrules and Steel Cap.

3 Pieces .. 19/-
5 ,, .. 30/-

0988.

Silver Fancy Ferrules and Nickel Silver Caps.

3 Pieces .. 21/-
5 ,, .. 34/-

Above Carving sets in silver and electro-plate from Joseph Elliot, *c.* 1930.

Opposite Tea and luncheon baskets, and cutlery canteens from Mappin & Webb, 1909.

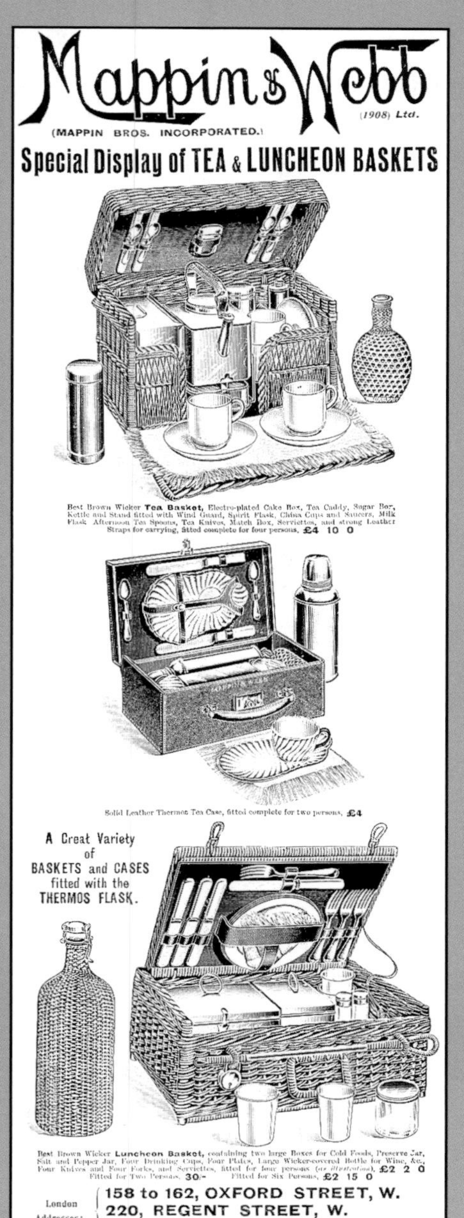
Mappin & Webb
(1908) Ltd.
(MAPPIN BROS. INCORPORATED.)
Special Display of TEA & LUNCHEON BASKETS
Best Brown Wicker Tea Basket, Electro-plated Cake Box, Tea Caddy, Sugar Box, Kettle and Stand fitted with Wind Guard, Spirit Flask, China Cups and Saucers, Milk Flask Afternoon Tea Spoons, Tea Knives, Match Box, Serviettes, and strong Leather Straps for carrying, fitted complete for four persons, £4 10 0
Solid Leather Thermos Tea Case, fitted complete for two persons, £4
A Great Variety of BASKETS and CASES fitted with the THERMOS FLASK.
Best Brown Wicker Luncheon Basket, containing two large Boxes for Cold Foods, Preserve Jar, Salt and Pepper Jar, Four Drinking Cups, Four Plates, Large Wicker-covered Bottle for Wine, &c., Four Knives and Four Forks, and Serviettes, fitted for four persons (as illustration), £2 2 0
Fitted for Two Persons, 30/- Fitted for Six Persons, £2 15 0
London Addresses:
158 to 162, OXFORD STREET, W.
220, REGENT STREET, W.
2, QUEEN VICTORIA ST., CITY (Opposite the Mansion House).
Paris: 1, RUE DE LA PAIX.
Sheffield. Manchester. Nice. Biarritz. Johannesburg.

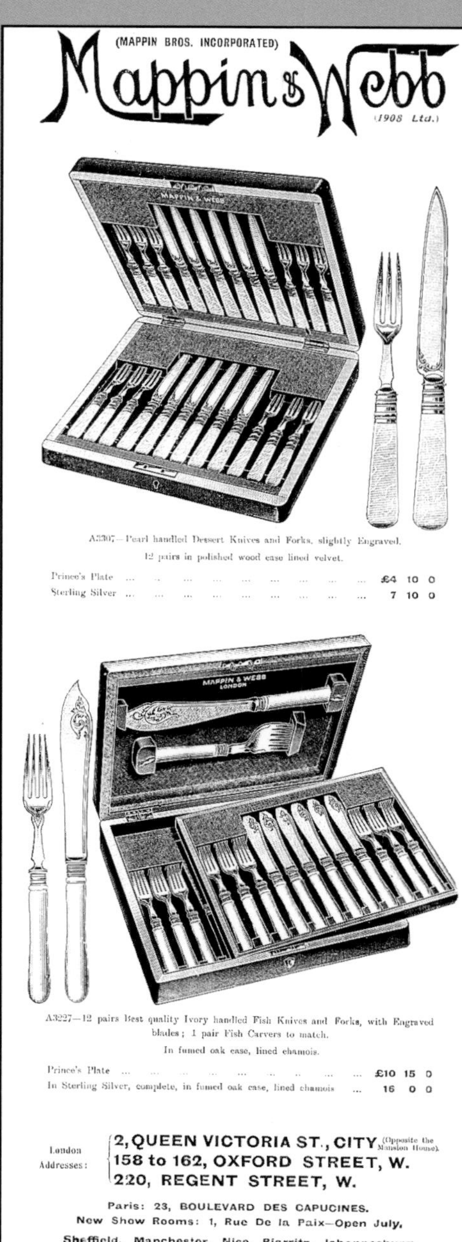
(MAPPIN BROS. INCORPORATED)
Mappin & Webb
(1908 Ltd.)
MAPPIN & WEBB
A3307—Pearl handled Dessert Knives and Forks, slightly Engraved.
12 pairs in polished wood case lined velvet.
Prince's Plate ... £4 10 0
Sterling Silver ... 7 10 0
MAPPIN & WEBB LONDON
A3227—12 pairs Best quality Ivory handled Fish Knives and Forks, with Engraved blades; 1 pair Fish Carvers to match.
In fumed oak case, lined chamois.
Prince's Plate ... £10 15 0
In Sterling Silver, complete, in fumed oak case, lined chamois ... 16 0 0
London Addresses:
2, QUEEN VICTORIA ST., CITY (Opposite the Mansion House).
158 to 162, OXFORD STREET, W.
220, REGENT STREET, W.
Paris: 23, BOULEVARD DES CAPUCINES.
New Show Rooms: 1, Rue De la Paix—Open July.
Sheffield. Manchester. Nice. Biarritz. Johannesburg.

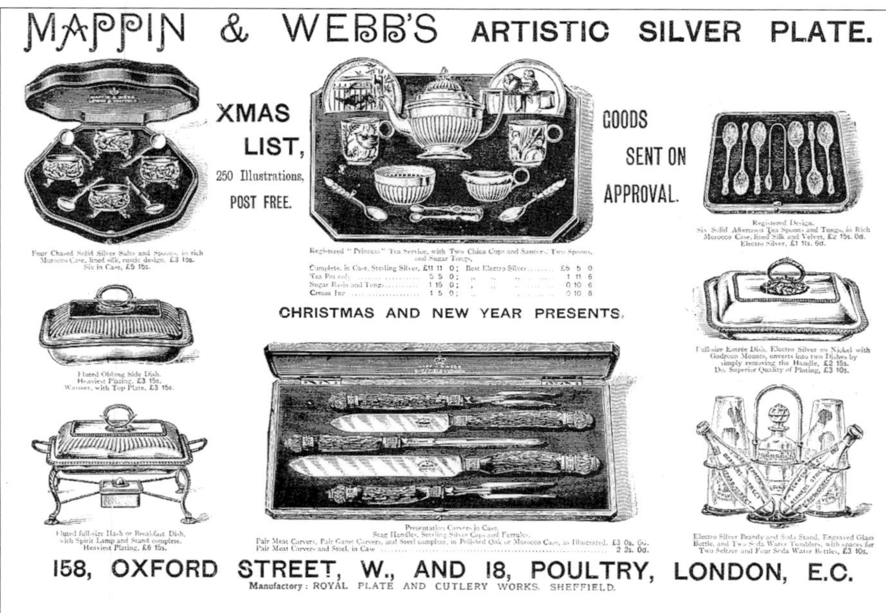

Above From Mappin & Webb's 'Christmas List', 1895.

Opposite and *below* China designs: Powell, Bishop & Stonier's sales catalogue, 1891.

MESSAGERIES MARITIMES

1re Classe le 189

PAQUEBOT

DÉJEUNER

HORS-D'ŒUVRE

PLATS DE CUISINE

DESSERT

CAFÉ

Opposite Menu card for an ocean voyage: chromolithograph, *c.* 1890.

Below Bill of fare for the first meal of the day aboard ship, 1863!

DINNER.

	ROAST.	BOILED.
Soups........		
Dishes Fish		
Do. Beef		
Do. Mutt...		

...SSORTED.

...do.
Rice do.
Pancakes.
Omelettes.

BILL OF FARE.

BRITISH AND NORTH AMERICAN
ROYAL MAIL STEAM SHIPS.

"Africa" 25th Day of June 1863

BREAKFAST.

Dishes of Beef-Steaks.
Do. Mutton Chops.
Do. Pork Chops.
Do. Veal Cutlets.
Do. Smoked Salmon.
Do. Broiled Chicken.
Do. Fried Ham.
Do. Cold Meats.
Do. Stews.
Eggs in Omelettes.
Do. Boiled.
Hominy.
Mush.

Preceding pages 'Dr Syntax at Vauxhall Gardens': copper engraving by George Cruikshank, *c.* 1820.

These pages Designs for china tableware from Powell, Bishop & Stonier's sales catalogue, 1891.

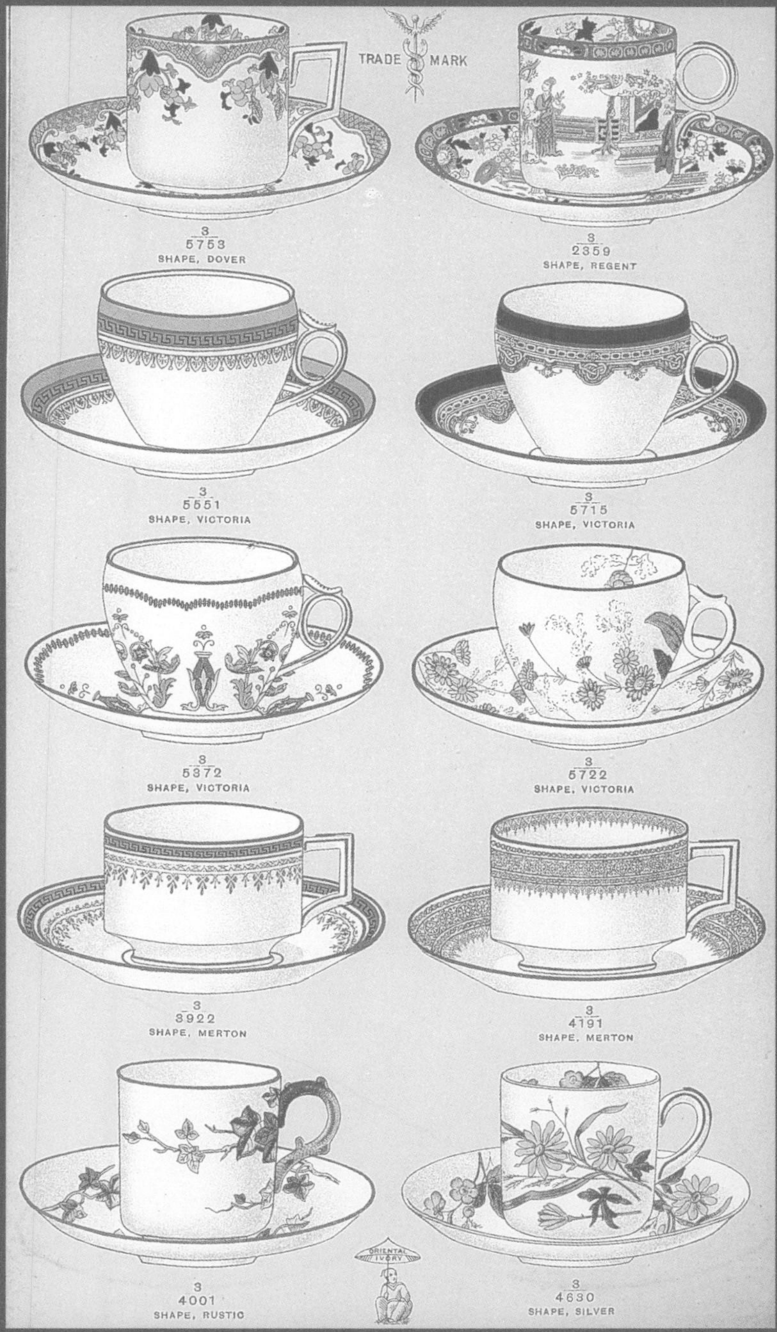
TRADE MARK
3
5753
SHAPE, DOVER
3
2359
SHAPE, REGENT
3
5551
SHAPE, VICTORIA
3
5715
SHAPE, VICTORIA
3
5372
SHAPE, VICTORIA
3
5722
SHAPE, VICTORIA
3
3922
SHAPE, MERTON
3
4191
SHAPE, MERTON
ORIENTAL IVORY
3
4001
SHAPE, RUSTIC
3
4630
SHAPE, SILVER

Above Acquiring the best for the table – an elegant shopper in a market arcade: tinted lithograph, Berlin, *c.* 1840.

Opposite Frederick II of Prussia entertaining guests at the palace of Sanssouci: photogravure print after an original painting by Menzel, Germany, late nineteenth century.

The laying of the banquet at the Guildhall, London, for Lord Mayor's Day: copper engraving from *The Gentleman's Magazine*, 1761.

Above 'Last at Table': illustration by M. Stretch from *The Illustrated Sporting and Dramatic News*, Christmas Number, 1883.

Opposite 'The Bachelor's Christmas Dinner': wood engraving by W. Thomas from *The Illustrated London News*, 1865.

W. THOMAS, Sc.

These pages Culinary ephemera: two graphic menu cards, *c.* 1880, and a Victorian sheet music cover with gastronomic themes.

Overleaf 'British Cooks Cramming Old Grumble-Gizzard' – Horatio Nelson and his fellow admirals serve up a victory feast to John Bull: copper engraving by James Gillray, 1798.

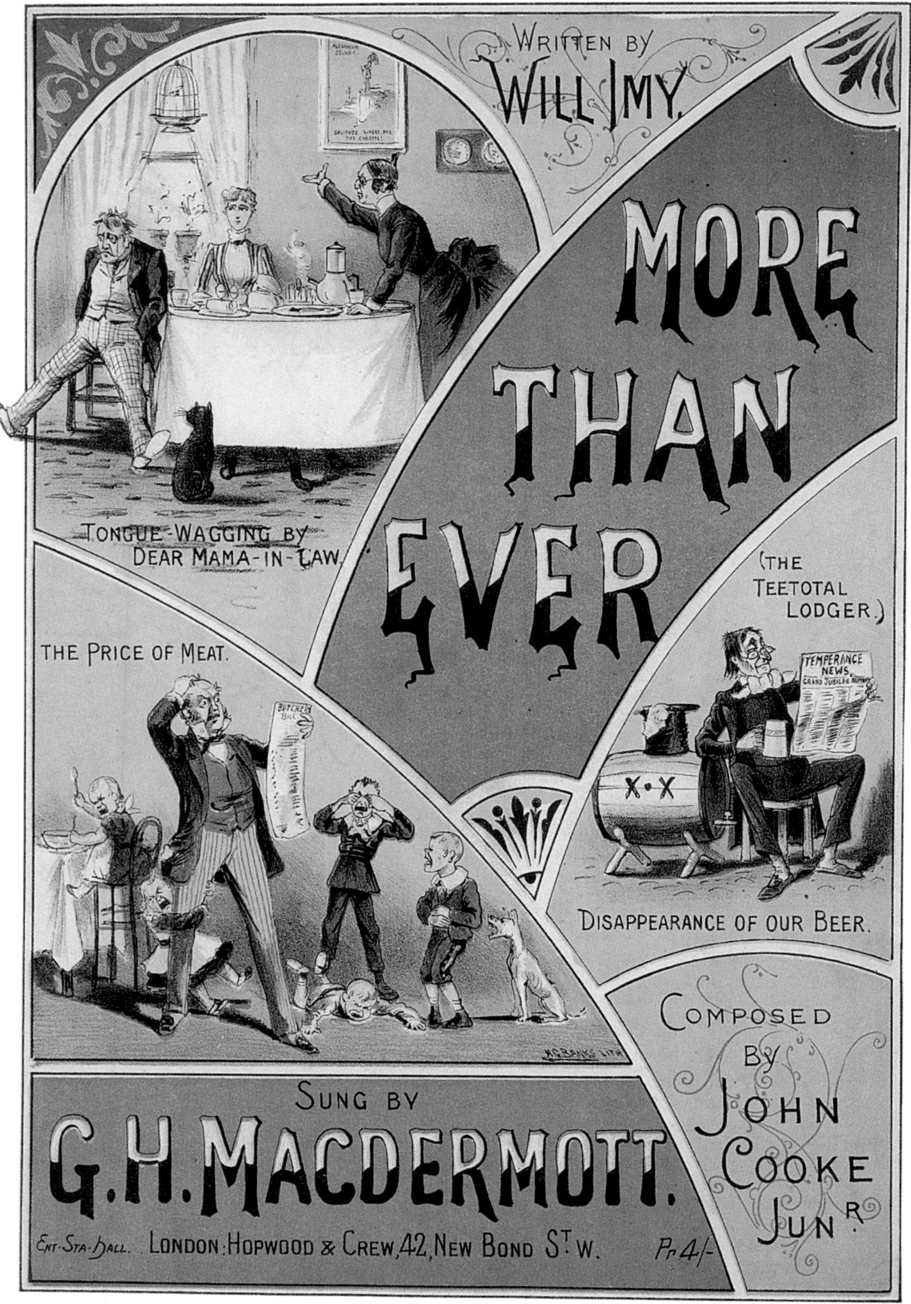
WRITTEN BY
WILL IMY.
MORE THAN EVER
TONGUE-WAGGING BY DEAR MAMA-IN-LAW.
THE PRICE OF MEAT.
(THE TEETOTAL LODGER.)
TEMPERANCE NEWS.
X·X
DISAPPEARANCE OF OUR BEER.
COMPOSED BY JOHN COOKE JUNR.
SUNG BY
G.H. MACDERMOTT.
ENT-STA-HALL. LONDON: HOPWOOD & CREW, 42, NEW BOND ST. W. Pr 4/-

What! more Frigasees?—why you sons o'bitches, you, where do ye think I shall find room to stow all you bring in?
Nelson
BUONAPARTE in EGYPT
Curse his Guts, he'll take a chop at Us, next

a la BRIDPORT
Fricando à la HOWE
Fricassée à la NELSON
DUTCH Cheese
DUTCH Cheese
a la DUNCAN
List of French Ships Taken Burnt & destro
True British Stout.

Compote of Pine.

Dish of Plums.

Dish of Strawberries.

Iced Oranges.

Raspberry Ices.

Centre Dish of Various Fruits.

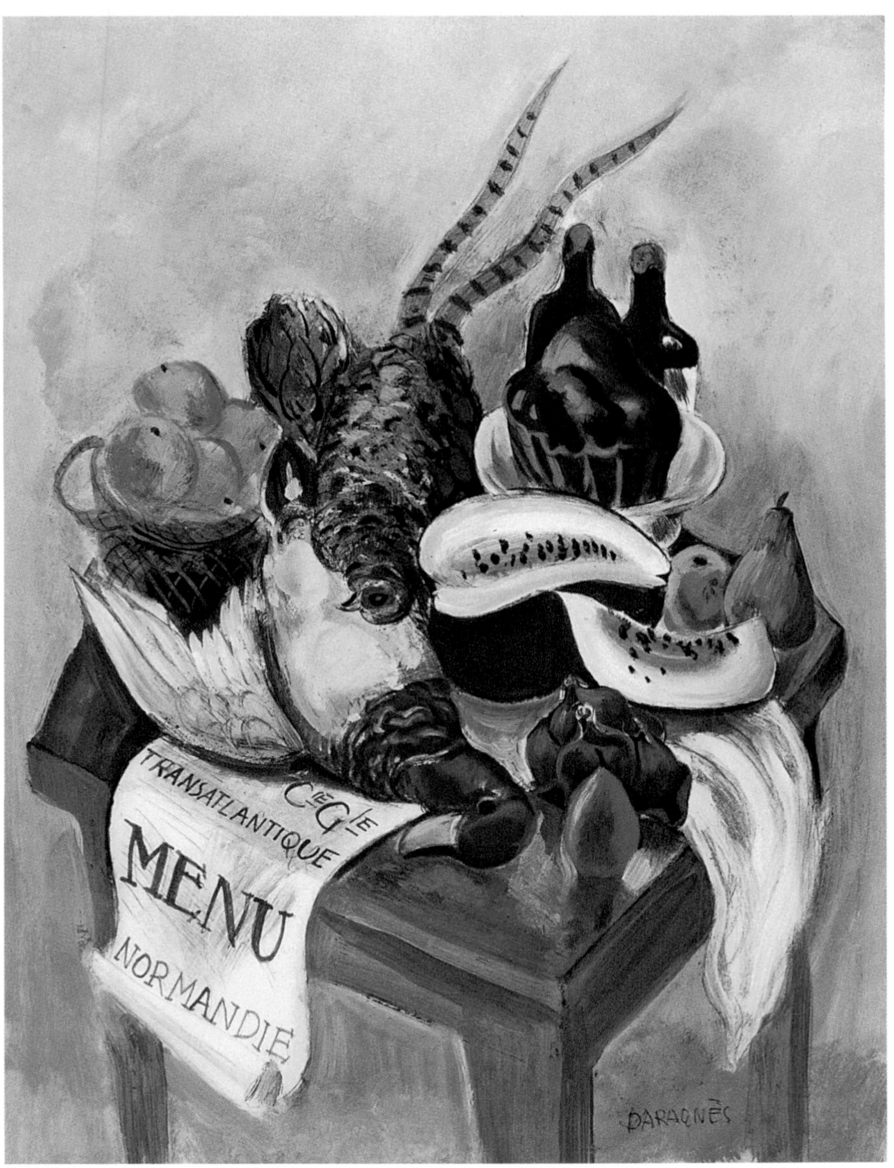

Opposite The final touch: a selection of delights from the second edition of *Mrs. Beeton's Book of Household Management*, London, 1869.

Page 325 Cover design for the bill of fare aboard the famous French liner *Normandie*, 1939: design by Jean-Gabriel Daragnès.

'The Christmas Pie and the Great Boar's Head': engraving from *The Illustrated Times*, 1857. 'A goodly procession is that in which these two chivalrous dishes are the chief actors, borne, as they are, on the shoulders of Royal footmen, blazing in scarlet and gold lace.'

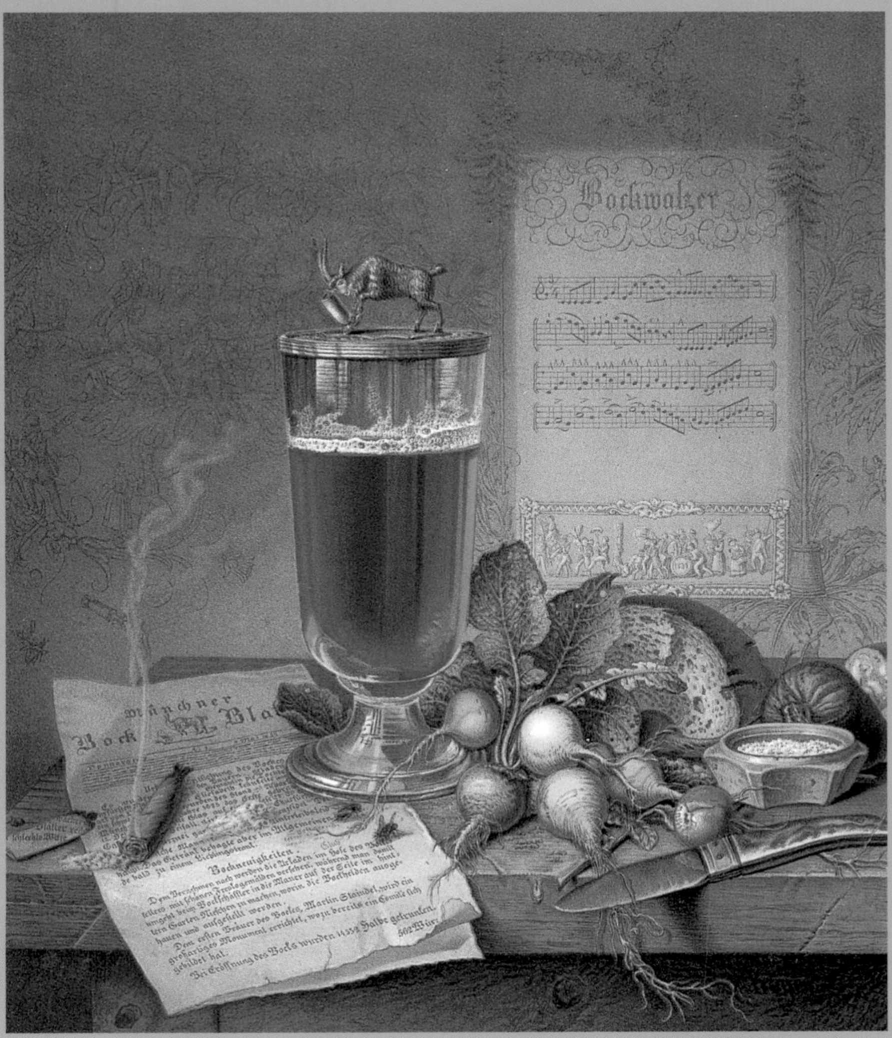

Opposite Desserts from Jules Gouffé's *Le Livre de cuisine*, Paris, 1867.

Above Still-life of a glass of Bockbier and its accompaniment: chromolithograph after J. W. Preyer, Germany, *c.* 1860.

Above At the Hôtel des Princes – a dinner party in a private room of the hotel: steel engraving, Germany, *c.* 1845.

Opposite A traditional Turkish meal: copper engraving, eighteenth century.

CONGRÈS DE MONACO
1897
MENU
Hors-d'Œuvre variés
Saumon froid
Sauces Tartare et Gribiche
Filet de Bœuf à la Monégasque
Cailles en Chaufroid
Poulardes à la Souwaroff
Salade Printanière
Asperges de Vaucluse
Sauce Mousseline
Bombes Norwégiennes
Pâtisserie
Vins
Médoc — Chablis — Saint-Emilion
Champagne rafraichi
Jeudi 22 Avril
BANQUET
Offert à l'Association Littéraire et Artistique Internationale
Restaurant du Righi d'Hiver
La Turbie

Opposite Menu for L'Association Littéraire et Artistique Internationale, Monaco, 1897.

This page Conserves Seethal menu card, *c.* 1920; a first-class lunch menu from a steamship, 1901.

Parson Curtis's dinner party – 'roasted and brought to table': lithograph by H. Alben, *c.* 1840.

Leg of Mutton with Haricot Beans.
Calf's Ears à la Financière.
Filets of Beef larded.
Lamb Cutlets with Green Peas.
Veal Cutlets aux Olives.
Pig's Feet with Truffles.
PL. IV

Left Savoury dishes from the second edition of *Mrs. Beeton's Book of Household Management*, 1869.

Below A traditional late Victorian dinner setting with massive floral centrepiece: chromolithograph, *c.* 1880.

ii—SUPPLEMENT TO THE ILLUSTRATED LONDON

SAVING THEIR SERVANTS AND ENJOYING THEMSELVES WITH

From the Painting by A. C. Mi

GIVING THEIR HOUSEHOLDS A REST: DINING-OUT AT A F

To dine in a famous restaurant, or a great hotel, on Sunday has become a habit with very many Society people, and there can be no doubt that in a considerable number of instan they are enabled thus to give their servan

NSCIENCES: SOCIETY'S SUNDAY EVENING.

N RESTAURANT—THE BERKELEY.

ted to the new mode not only by charm of surroundings, with excellence of cooking and service, but by the fact that

Left A likely story! Society people are attracted to dining-out not only by their surroundings but also by the opportunity to give their servants a rest: colour print from *The Illustrated London News*, 1912.

Overleaf 'The Merriest Method of Bringing in the New Year' – the scene at The Savoy 'was one of the gayest imaginable, as the company sang *Auld Lang Syne* the heart of Robert Burns in the adjoining gardens on The Embankment must almost have come to life in its bronze casement...': colour print after René Lelong from *The Graphic*, 3 January, 1914.

'The Health of the Bride' – a modest wedding feast: illustration after a painting by Stanhope A. Forbes, 1890, from *The Graphic*, 1900.

A family banquet, eighteenth-century style: mezzotint by Johann-Jakob Haid, Augsburg, *c.* 1750.

Fish day at the abbey: menu designed and engraved by Georges Thouvenot for the forty-sixth dinner of Les Compagnons de la Belle Table, 16 March 1955.

The *pièce de résistance – tête de veau*: chromolithograph from Gouffé's *Le Livre de cuisine*, Paris, 1867.

SPES
Banquet organisat per
la colonia catalana de Ma-
drid en homenatje als Srs.
Ventosa, Rodés, Marqués
de Camps i Ferrer i Vidal.
Menu
Melon Cocktail
Marmita Henry IV.
Filets de Sole Castiglione
Mignonntte de Veau-
au Beurre.
Pommes de Virginie.
Petits Pois a la Francaise
Suprêmes de Perdreaux
aux Truffes fraiches.
Sorbet à la Mandarinnette
Poularde Rôtie Americaine.
Salade Criole
Fruits d'Amour Alexandre
Mignardises – Moka
Miguel Blay
Vins
Morales Burgos – Sauternes en
Carafe – Château Margaux 1899
– Champagne Brut Imperial,
Moët & Chandon – Liqueurs
– Eaux Minerales – Cigares –
4 Desembre 1917 – Hotel Ritz
S. Gerona

Above Menu card for a banquet for the Catalan community of Madrid, 1917.

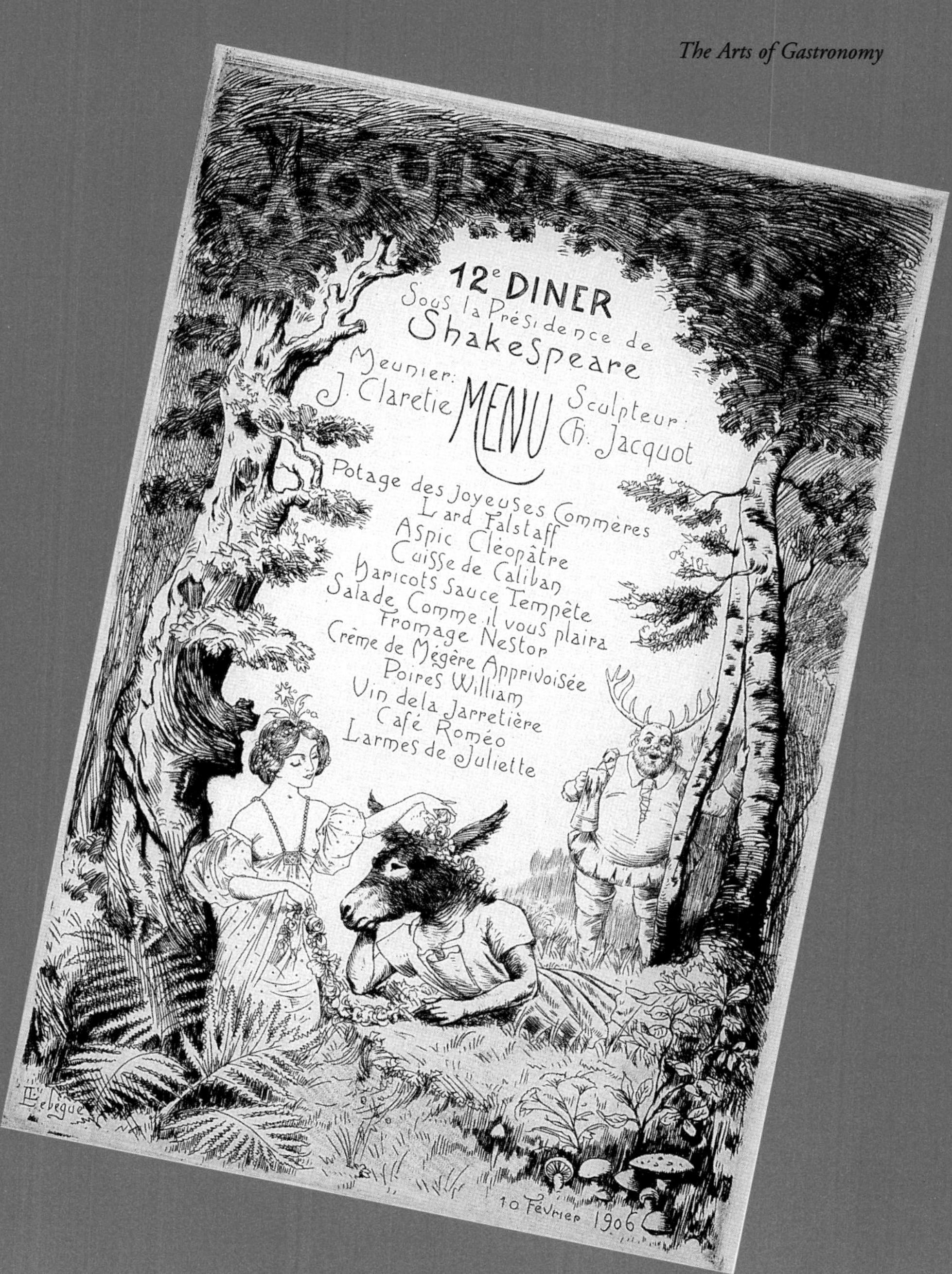

Above Dining club menu card on themes from Shakespeare's plays, 1906.

BECASSE
AUG. MICHEL
STRASBOURG
DEUTZ & GELDERMANN
MICHEL
MENU
TERRINE
AUG. MICHEL
STRASBOURG
DEUTZ & GELDERMANN
GOLD LACK
MENU

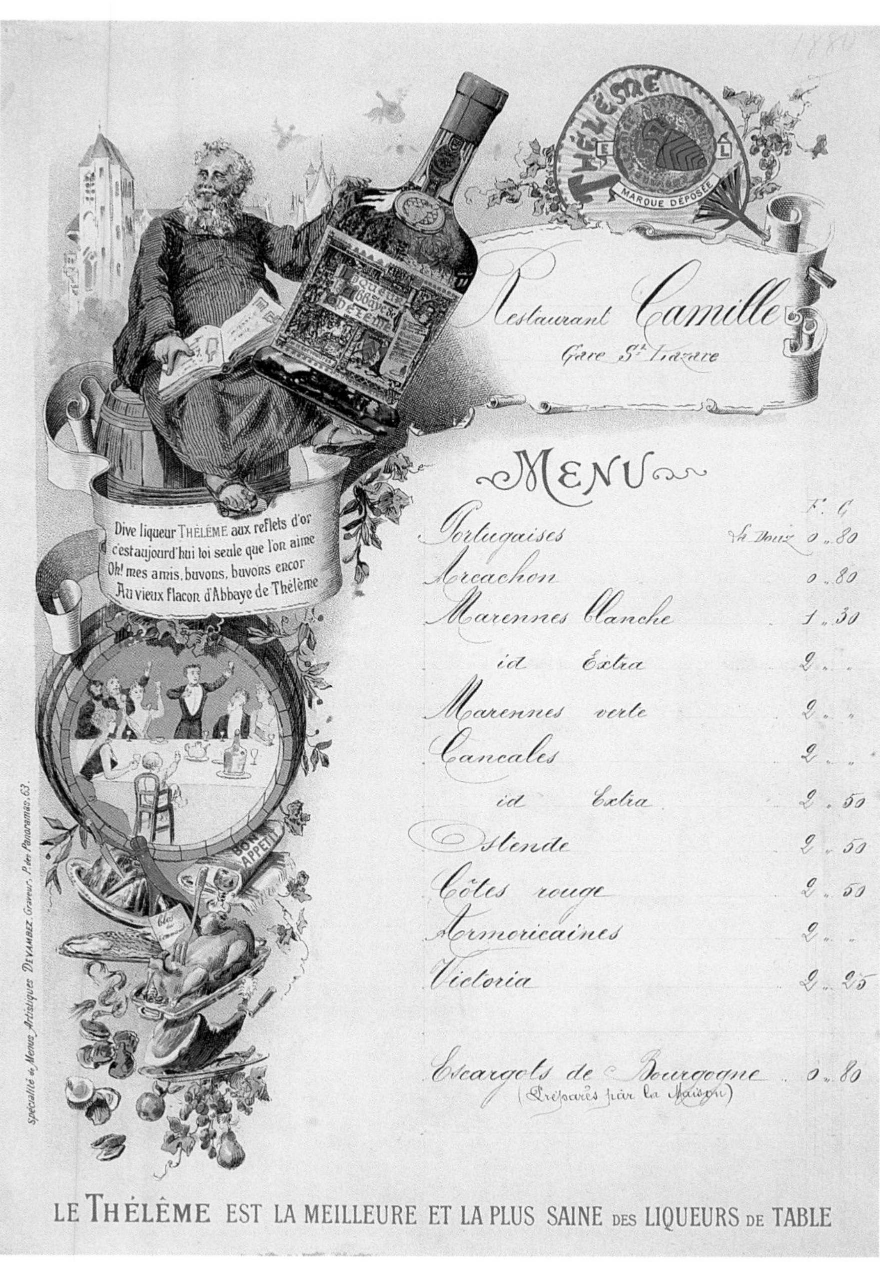

Opposite and *above* Various French advertising menu cards, *c.* 1880.

Opposite The Mayor's banquet in the Guildhall of York: wood engraving from *The Illustrated London News*, 1873.

Above Menu cover designed and engraved by Pierre Brissand for the forty-first dinner of Les Compagnons de la Belle Table, 1954.

MESSAGERIES MARITIMES
1re Classe
le 16 Janvier 1897
PAQUEBOT Cordillère
DÉJEUNER
HORS-D'ŒUVRE
Beurre, Radis
Olives noires
Viande froide
PLATS DE CUISINE
Omelette fines herbes
Poisson frit
Foie à l'Italienne
Romsteck aux pommes
Tourterelles
DESSERT
Port Salut, chester
Pêches, prunes
Biscuits
CAFÉ
IMP. MARSEILLAISE, R. SAINTE, 39.
MOD. N° 49.

These pages Various menu cards, from that of a cross-Channel ferry, 1897 *(opposite)*, to advertisements for Dubouché cognac, *c.* 1910 *(above)*, and *(right)* a Jugendstil design for the Hotel Marquart in Stuttgart, *c.* 1903.

JELLIES
CHOCOLATES
TEA
COFFEE
WINES

ICES
SOUPS
JELLIES
BALL
SUPPERS

Preceding pages A fashionable tea-shop: colour print by F. D. Bedford, *c.* 1900.

These pages 'Shame on you, grim old bachelors, who sit so moody there! Why, don't you know 'tis Christmas Eve?': wood engraving by Swain after a painting by F. Barnard, from *The Illustrated London News*, 1889.

Below Lawyers at lunch – scene in a restaurant near the Paris law courts: drawn from life by Charles-Paul Rénouard, *c.* 1890.

Above Afternoon tea in Regent Street: drawn by Mary L. Gow for *The Graphic*, Summer Number, 1893.

Above 'A Raid on the Dessert': colour print after a painting by E. K. Johnson, from *The Graphic*, Christmas Number, 1885.

Opposite above 'Preparing for a Nightmare': colour print from *The Graphic*, Christmas Number, 1878.

Opposite below 'Who Takes the Cake?': chromolithograph after a painting by Fanny Moody, 1891.

THE NIGHT SIDE OF NATURE

THE ILLUSTRATED LONDON NEWS.

REGISTERED AT THE GENERAL POST-OFFICE FOR TRANSMISSION ABROAD.

No. 2156.—VOL. LXXVII. SATURDAY, SEPTEMBER 25, 1880. WITH TWO SUPPLEMENTS } SIXPENCE. BY POST, 6½D.

Opposite 'A Young Ladies' School of Cookery': wood engraving from *The Illustrated London News*, 1880.

Above More designs for china tableware from Powell, Bishop & Stonier's sales catalogue, 1891.

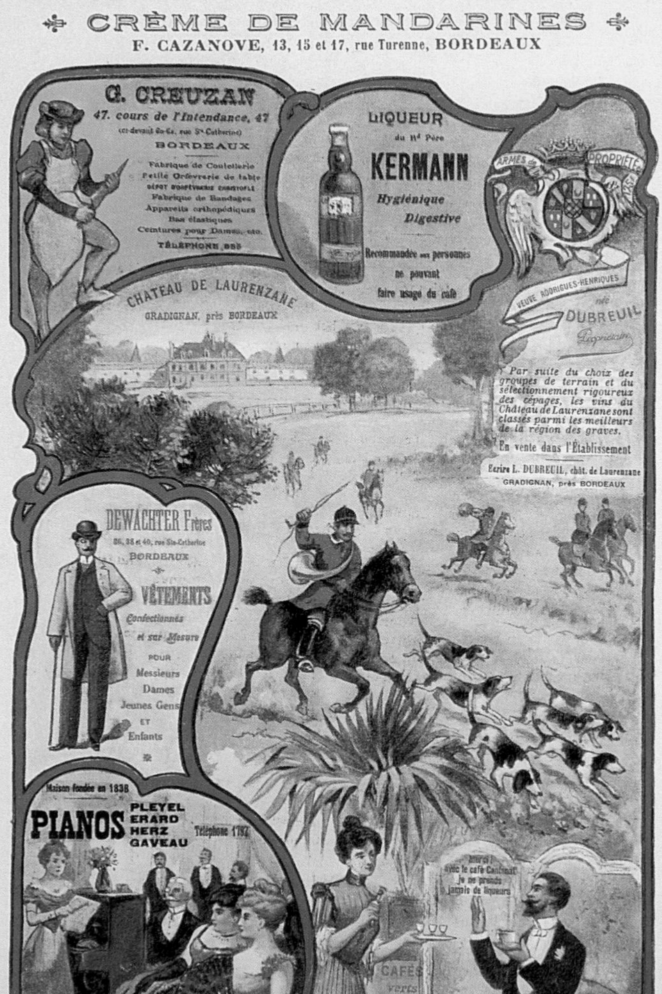

These pages A French menu and a *carte des vins*, with local advertising, *c.* 1900.

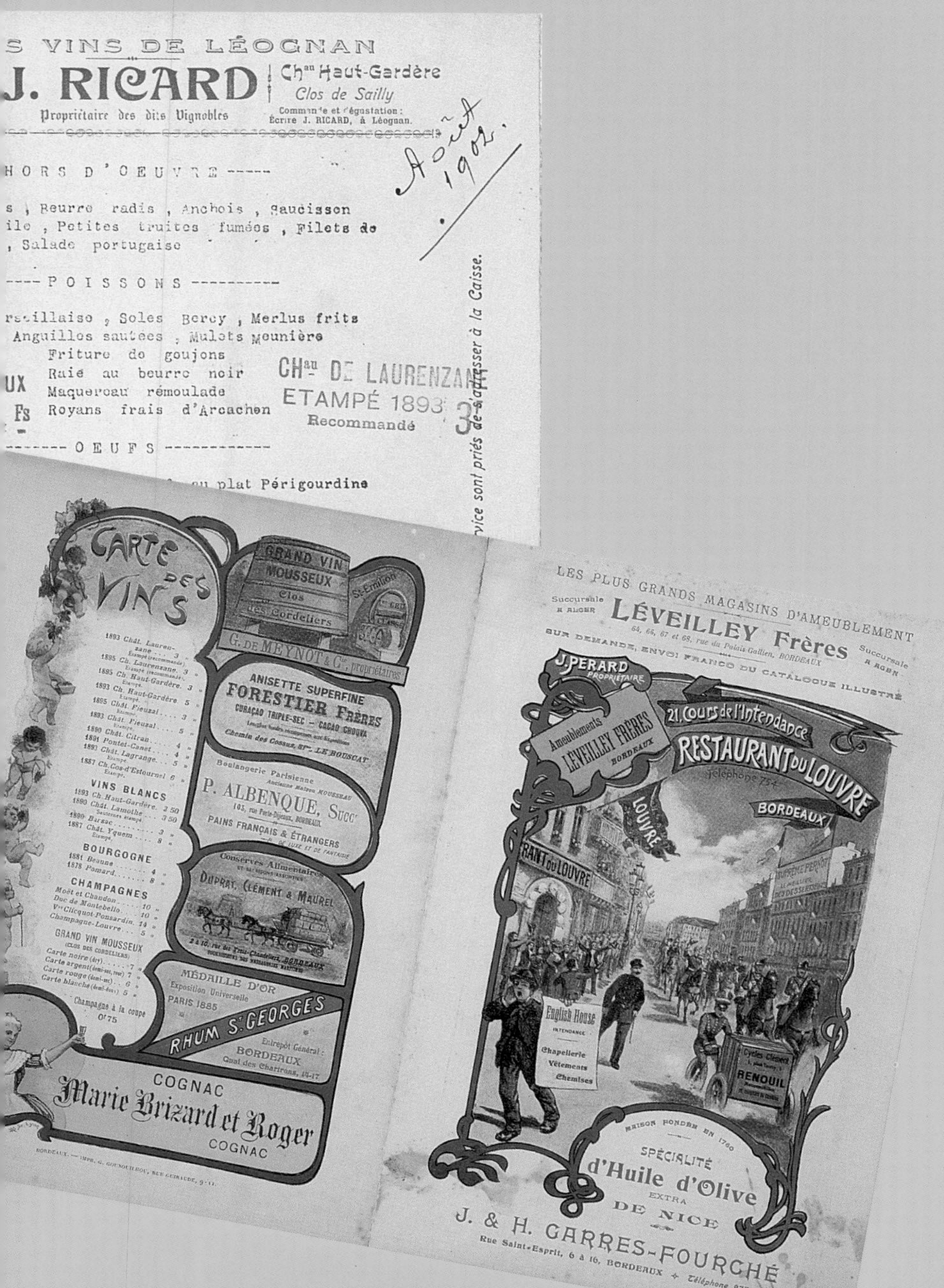
S VINS DE LÉOGNAN
J. RICARD
Propriétaire des dits Vignobles
Chau Haut-Gardère
Clos de Sailly
Écrire J. RICARD, à Léognan.
Août 1902.
HORS D'OEUVRE
s , Beurre radis , Anchois , Saucisson
ile , Petites truites fumées , Filets de
, Salade portugaise
POISSONS
rseillaise , Soles Bercy , Merlus frits
Anguilles sautées , Mulets meunière
Friture de goujons
Raie au beurre noir
Maquereau rémoulade
Royans frais d'Arcachon
CHau DE LAURENZANE
ETAMPÉ 1893
Recommandé
OEUFS
au plat Périgourdine
vice sont priés de s'adresser à la Caisse.
CARTE DES VINS
VINS BLANCS
BOURGOGNE
CHAMPAGNES
GRAND VIN MOUSSEUX
Champagne à la coupe
GRAND VIN MOUSSEUX
Clos des Cordeliers
G. DE MEYNOT & Cie, propriétaires
ANISETTE SUPERFINE
FORESTIER FRÈRES
CURAÇAO TRIPLE-SEC — CACAO CHOUVA
Boulangerie Parisienne
P. ALBENQUE, Succr
PAINS FRANÇAIS & ÉTRANGERS
Conserves Alimentaires
DUPRAT, CLÉMENT & MAUREL
MÉDAILLE D'OR
Exposition Universelle
PARIS 1885
RHUM St GEORGES
BORDEAUX
COGNAC
Marie Brizard et Roger
COGNAC
LES PLUS GRANDS MAGASINS D'AMEUBLEMENT
LÉVEILLEY Frères
SUR DEMANDE, ENVOI FRANCO DU CATALOGUE ILLUSTRÉ
J. PERARD
PROPRIÉTAIRE
Ameublements LÉVEILLEY FRÈRES BORDEAUX
21, Cours de l'Intendance
RESTAURANT DU LOUVRE
BORDEAUX
English House
Chapellerie
Vêtements
Chemises
RENOUIL
MAISON FONDÉE EN 1760
SPÉCIALITÉ
d'Huile d'Olive
EXTRA
DE NICE
J. & H. GARRES-FOURCHÉ
Rue Saint-Esprit, 6 à 16, BORDEAUX Téléphone 977

Opposite 'La Tentation' – a modern Adam and Eve: illustration by Paul Iribe promoting Les Établissements Nicolas, 1930.

Below 'The Oyster Feast': wood engraving by Evald Hansen after a painting by Carl-Gustaf Hellquist, Paris, 1884.

NICOLAS
CARTE DES VINS
PAUL IRIBE
LA TENTATION

COTON
Bertall

Preceding pages The *table d'hôte*: copper engraving by Isaac Cruikshank, 1796.

Opposite *'L'Obésité et la maigreur'*: illustration by Bertall in a 1848 edition of Brillat-Savarin's *La Physiologie du goût*, originally published in 1825.

Above The hungry hunter: illustration from *Les Classiques de la Table*, Paris, 1844.

MONACO

BUFFET DU 23 AVRIL 1897

Consommé chaud
Consommé froid
Saumon — Langoustes
Chaufroix de Poulets, Ortolans et Cai
Filet de Bœuf à la G
Galantine et Poulet
Terrines de Fo
Jambon hist
Langue écarla
Salade Rus
Salade d'Haric

SANDWICHES

Notre devise est
TOUJOURS A MIEUX
comme notre nom
AMIEUX-FRÈRES
CHAMPIGNONS & TOUTES CONSERVES

MENU

du Mardi Gras
1903.
Hors d'oeuvre variés.
Tête de veau nature
Cassolettes de ris de veau
Canard rouennais
Fonds d'artichauts Lucullus
Salade de saison.
Gateau diplomate
Fruits - Desserts.

Imp. H. Laas, E. Pécaud & Cie, Paris.

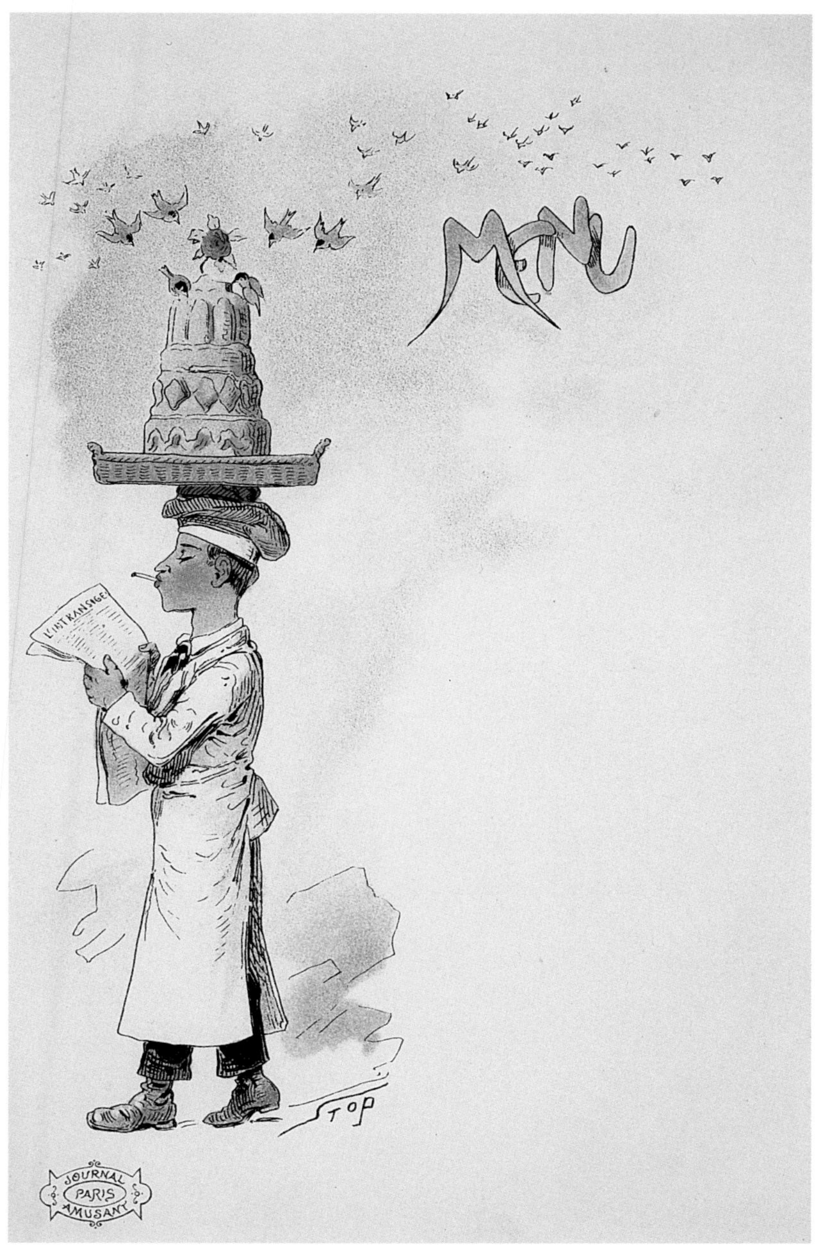

These pages By the late nineteenth century the restaurants in Paris had become accepted centres of social life, accompanied by the elegant art of the menu card.

Les Trois Frères Provençaux – the celebrated restaurant in the Palais Royal, Paris: steel engraving by J. B. Allen after a painting by Eugène Lami, *c.* 1850.

"May I press you to a jelly?"

These pages Sex and food: seduction by the sweets of the table, *c.* 1925; 'gilded bohemia', New Year's Eve at the Pré-Catalan, *c.* 1900.

WE
PRAISE GOD
&
THANK YOU

Preceding pages Dinner of the Royal Humane Society in the Freemasons' Hall: steel engraving by H. Melville after a drawing by T. H. Shepherd, *c.* 1840.

Opposite More from Mrs. Beeton – savoury dishes: second edition of her *Book of Household Management*, 1869.

Above and *right* Traditional French costumes illustrated on menu cards advertising biscuits.

Savoury Jelly à la Belle-Vue.

Chaud-froid of Fowl with Savoury Jelly.

Pheasants à la Financière.

Casserole of potatoes with Rabbit and Truffles.

Casserole of Rice with hashed Game.

Crumbs from the rich man's table – distributing food to the poor at the Guildhall after the Lord Mayor's Banquet: wood engraving after a painting by Adrien Marie, from *The Graphic*, 1883.

DELICIEUSES A LA MONACO
CHATEAU LEOVILLE 1870

SAUMON St-JACQUES A LA MARINIERE
HOCHHEIMER 1865

JAMBON DE PRAGUE A LA CHIPOLATA
CHATEAU LAFITTE 1870

SUPREMES DE CAILLES A LA GODARD

MACEDOINE DE FILETS DE VOLAILLES
CHATEAU GRILLET 1874

Sorbets au Champagne

FILET DE CHEVREUIL A LA St-HUBERT
CLOS DE VOUGEOT 1865

CANETONS TRUFFES A L'ECOSSAISE
ROMANEE CONTI 1865

LANGOUSTES A LA PARISIENNE
CHATEAU YQUEM 1869

GATEAU MONTMORENCY

BOUQUET DE GLACES

FRUITS — DESSERT
TOKAY ROYAL 1858

These pages Shellfish heaven: a menu card of 1904, and a *buisson de coquillages* from Jules Gouffé's *Le Livre de cuisine*, Paris, 1867.

Dinner of the Dilettanti Society at the Thatched House Club: steel engraving by J. H. Le Keux after T. H. Shepherd, *c.* 1829.

Overleaf Some final touches from Jules Gouffé: lobster salad, followed by filet steaks and mayonnaise.

MENU
Déjeuner du "CORNET"
LUNDI 5 NOVEMBRE 1900
Hors d'œuvre
Raie au beurre noir
Tripes à la Mode de Caen
Rumpsteak pommes à l'anglaise
Entremets
Fromages
Desserts
Café cognac
46e repas du Cornet

Bibliography

The following list of books and other publications is, perforce, partial and highly individual; a comprehensive bibliography of the description and illustration of food matters would be well beyond the scope of the present volume. What follows is essentially a listing of those works which have either provided us with material for reproduction in the foregoing sections of this book or inspired us in some way during its preparation.

The Accomplish'd Housewife or, The Gentlewoman's Companion, London, 1745.

Acton, Eliza, *Modern Cookery for Private Families*, London, 1875.

Albert, B., *Le Cuisinier Parisien*, Paris, 1828.

Audot, Louis-Eustache, *La Cuisinière de la campagne et de la ville*, Paris, 1827.

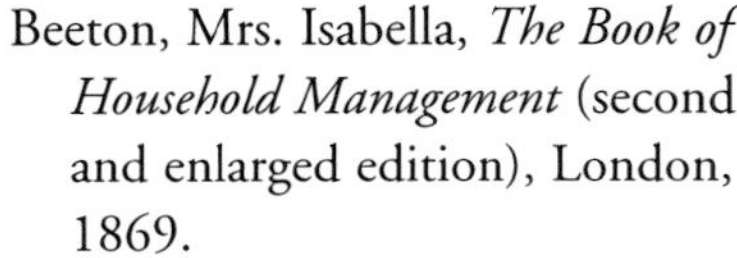

Beeton, Mrs. Isabella, *The Book of Household Management* (second and enlarged edition), London, 1869.

Blome, Richard, *The Gentleman's Recreation*, London, 1686.

Briggs, Richard, *The English Art of Cookery*, London, 1794.

Brillat-Savarin, Jean-Anthelme, *La Physiologie du goût*, edition illustrated by Bertall, Paris, 1848, originally published 1825.

Brookshaw, George, *Pomona Britannica*, London, 1804–12.

Bull, Henry George, *The Herefordshire Pomona*, London & Hereford, 1876–85.

Two contrary landlords – 'If you WANT you may have, WHAT MORE would you crave?': etching, *c.* 1800.

Butterworth, Benjamin, *The Growth of Industrial Art*, Washington, 1892.

Carême, Antonin, *Le Cuisinier Parisien*, Paris, 1854.

Carter, Charles, *The Compleat City and Country Cook*, London, 1732.

Les Classiques de la Table, Paris, 1844.

Collingwood, Francis and Woolams, John, *The Universal Cook, and City and Country Housekeeper*, London, 1797.

Copley, Esther, *The Housekeeper's Guide*, London, 1834.

Curtis, William, *The Botanical Magazine*, London, 1790–1800.

Dods, Mistress Margaret (= Mrs. C. J. Johnstone), *The Cook and Housewife's Manual*, Edinburgh, 1864.

Encyclopedia Londiniensis, or The Universal Dictionary of Arts, Sciences and Literature, London, 1810–29.

The Family Cookery Book, London, 1840.

Farley, John, *The London Art of Cookery*, London, 1811.

The Farmer's Wife, or The Complete Country Housewife, London, 1780.

Florinus, Franciscus Philippus (= F. P. von Sulzbach), *Œconomus Prudens et Legalis*, Nuremberg, 1702.

Francatelli, Charles Elmé, *The Modern Cook*, London, 1855.

Francke, Johann, *Veronica Theézans*, Leipzig and Coburg, 1700.

Frazer, Mrs., *The Practice of Cookery, Pastry, Confectionery, Pickling, Preserving, etc.*, Edinburgh, 1795.

The Gentleman's Magazine, and Historical Chronicle, London, 1761.

Gerarde, John, *The Herball or General Historie of Plantes*, London, 1597.

Goethe, Johann Wolfgang von, *Reinecke Fuchs*, illustrated edition, Munich, 1846.

Glasse, Hannah, *The Art of Cookery, Made Plain and Easy*, London, 1748.

Gouffé, Jules, *Le Livre de cuisine*, Paris, 1867.

Gouffé, Jules, *Le Livre des conserves*, Paris, 1869.

Gouffé, Jules, *Le Livre des soupes et des potages*, Paris, 1875.

Gouffé, Jules, *The Royal Book of Pastry and Confectionery (Le Livre de pâtisserie)*, London, 1874.

The Graphic, London, 1870–1910.

Grimod de la Reynière, Alexandre Balthazar Laurent, *Manuel des Amphitryons*, Paris, 1808.

Guégan, Bertrand, *La Fleur de la Cuisine Française*, Paris, 1921.

Harrison, Sarah, *The Housekeeper's Pocket-Book, and Compleat Family Cook*, London, 1777.

Henderson, William Augustus, *The Housekeeper's Instructor, or Universal Family Cook*, London, 1805.

Holland, Mary, *The Complete Economical Cook, and Frugal Housewife*, London, 1853.

Humelbergius Secundus, Dick, *Apician Morsels*, London, 1829.

The Illustrated London News, London, 1842–1900.

The Illustrated Sporting and Dramatic News, London, 1900.

The Illustrated Times, London, 1855–59.

Jacoutot, Auguste, *Chocolate and Confectionery Manufacture*, London, 1917.

Jenks, James, *The Complete Cook*, London, 1768.

Jennings, James, *Two Thousand Five Hundred Practical Recipes in Family Cookery*, London, 1837.

Jewry, Mary, *Warne's Model Cookery*, London and New York, 1899.

Kitchiner, William, *Apicius Redivivus, The Cook's Oracle*, London, 1818.

Kreetschmer, Albert, *Deutsche Volkstrachten*, Leipzig, 1870.

Lemery, Louis, *A Treatise of All Sorts of Foods*, London, 1745.

Liger, Louis, *Le Ménage des champs et de la ville*, Paris, 1738.

Llanover, Lady, *Good Cookery Illustrated*, London, 1867.

Lucas, Edward Verrall, *A Book of Shops*, London, 1899.

A gargantuan feast: chromolithograph published by Lemercier, Paris, *c.* 1860.

Macdonald, Duncan, *The New London Family Cook, or Town and Country Housekeeper's Guide*, London, 1800.

Marshall, Agnes B., *Mrs. A. B. Marshall's Larger Cookery Book of Extra Recipes*, London, 1902.

Massialot, Fr., *Le Cuisinier royal et bourgeois*, Paris, 1693.

Mayer, Johann, *Pomona Franconica*, Nuremberg, 1776.

Mellish, Katharine, *Katharine Mellish's Cookery and Domestic Management*, London and New York, 1901.

Melroe, Eliza, *An Economical and New Method of Cookery*, London, 1798.

Meyer's Universum, Hildburghausen, 1833–60.

Middleton, John, *Five Hundred New Receipts*, London, 1734.

The New London Cookery, and Complete Domestic Guide, London, 1827.

Newington, Thomas, *A Butler's Recipe Book 1719*, Cambridge, 1935.

Nicolas, Établissements, *Plaquettes 1–3*, Paris, 1930–32.

Nignon, Édouard, *Les Plaisirs de la table*, Paris, 1926.

Nott, John, *The Cook's and Confectioner's Dictionary*, London, 1726.

Nutt, Frederic, *The Complete Confectioner*, London, 1809.

Nutt, Frederic, *The Imperial and Royal Cook*, London, 1809.

Peckham, Ann, *The Complete English Cook*, Leeds, 1780.

Pelletier, Eugène and Auguste, *Le Thé et le chocolat dans l'alimentation publique*, Paris, 1861.

Petit Journal Pour Rire, Paris, 1856–70.

The Pictorial World, London, 1883.

Platina, Bartholomeus Sacchi de, *Von Allen Speisen und Gerichte*, Augsburg, 1530.

The Portfolio, An Artistic Periodical, London, 1870–86.

Powell, Bishop and Stonier, *Illustrated Catalogue of China and Earthenware*, Hanley, 1891.

Prévost d'exiles, Antoine François, *L'Histoire générale des voyages*, Paris, 1746–70.

Raffald, Elizabeth, *The Experienced English Housekeeper*, London, 1799.

Redouté, Pierre-Joseph, *Choix des plus belles fleurs et des plus beaux fruits*, Paris, 1827–33.

Rorer, Sarah Tyson, *Mrs. Rorer's Philadelphia Cook Book*, Philadelphia, 1886.

Royal and Universal Dictionary of Arts and Sciences, London, 1780.

Rumpolt, Markus, *Ein New Kochbuch*, Frankfurt-am-Main, 1604.

Rundell, Maria Eliza, *The New Family Receipt-Book*, London, 1820.

Rundell, Maria Eliza, *A New System of Domestic Cookery*, London, 1843.

Shepherd, Thomas Hosmer, *Metropolitan Improvements*, London, 1829.

Simpson, John, *A Complete System of Cookery*, London, 1816.

Smith, Eliza, *The Compleat Housewife, or Accomplish'd Gentlewoman's Companion*, London, 1734.

Soyer, Alexis, *The Modern Housewife or Ménagère*, London, 1850.

Soyer, Alexis, *The Pantropheon*, Boston, 1853.

Soyer, Alexis, *A Shilling Cookery for the People*, London and New York, 1855.

The Sphere: An Illustrated Newspaper for the Home, London, 1901–12.

Ude, Louis-Eustache, *The French Cook*, London, 1827.

Utrecht-Friedel, Louise Béate Augustine, *Le Confiseur impérial*, Paris, 1809.

Viard and Fouret, *Le Cuisinier royal*, Paris, 1820.

The Young Woman's Companion or, Frugal Housewife, Manchester, 1811.

Acknowledgments

During the years of our collecting, buying and selling books and prints of gastronomic interest we have formed many friendships and associations which we value. A number of people have been especially helpful in their suggestions concerning sources of the material of which this book is the distillation, and to them we extend our warmest thanks. One name, however, does deserve a very special mention: all the special photography of books, prints and other forms of imagery was carried out by the indefatigable and uncomplaining Julien Busselle to the highest possible standard.

Garwood & Voigt may be contacted at 55 Bayham Road, Sevenoaks, Kent TN13 3XE, England.
Tel: (01732) 460025; Fax: (01732) 460026;
Email: gv@garwood-voigt.com; Website: www.garwood-voigt.com

Overleaf The gherkin balloon – a mixed basket of contentious issues: cartoon in the *Lustige Blätter*, Germany, 1894.

Der Gurken-Ballon.

(Nach dem neuesten Modell der Militär-Luftschiffer-Abtheilung zu Berlin.)

Die saure Gurke — ehedem das Symbol der inhaltslosen Jahreszeit — erscheint diesmal am politischen Firmamente mit einer stattlichen Fracht der interessantesten Ereignisse.